Drawn & colored by Jodi Ho

Drawn by Laety Esperanza
Colored by CreaSam

## Global Doodle Gems Volume 16
"The Ultimate International Coloring Book...an epic Collection from Artists around the World !"

Drawn by Heba Seada & colored by Deb Norman

Drawn & colored by Judy West

Drawn & colored by Pica Wu

Drawn & colored by Gemeta Ling

Drawn & colored by Alison Civil

Drawn & colored by Tamara A Cameron

Drawn & colored by Nadege Zenfeerie

Drawn & colored by Kaloo Design

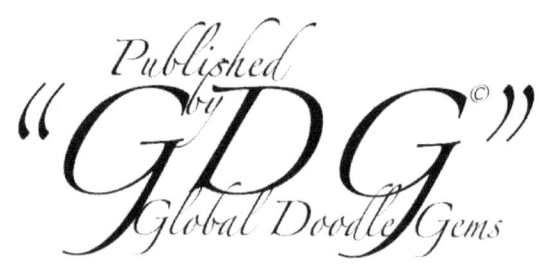

*Share your colored versions with us ! We love seeing your results and hearing from you we are social !*

The Official FB book page, stay on top of what we have in the works !
www.facebook.com/globaldoodlegems
The Community group, share your colored pages, meet the artists, enjoy exclusive freebies, take part in community Charity books and so much more......
www.facebook.com/groups/globaldoodlegems/
Follow us on Twitter.... @GlobalDoodlegem
We are on Instagram too
@globaldoodlegems for instagram
...and if you are not social like that we have a blog
globaldoodlegems.wordpress.com

Copyright © 2016 Global Doodle Gems
All rights are reserved by Global Doodle Gems.
Duplication of pages for personal use are allowed. You are invited to color the pages then scan/post your coloured versions to social networks, mentioning the book title and author/artist (Global Doodle Gems).
All artwork and images are protected by copyright laws. This book or any portion thereof may not, otherwise, be reproduced and/or distributed or transmitted without the express written permission of the artist/publisher of Global Doodle Gems.
All of us from the Global Doodle Gems wish you a colortastic time and look forward to seeing your wonderful color results online !

*Contributing Artists*

1. Nadege Zenfeerie
2. L'aety Esperanza
3. Alison Civil
4. Jodi Ho
5. Judy West
6. Tamara A. Cameron
7. Heba Seada
8. Pica Wu
9. Gemeta Ling
10. KaLoo Design

*Contributing Artist*
*Nadege Zenfeerie*
*France*

Facebook : zenfeerie

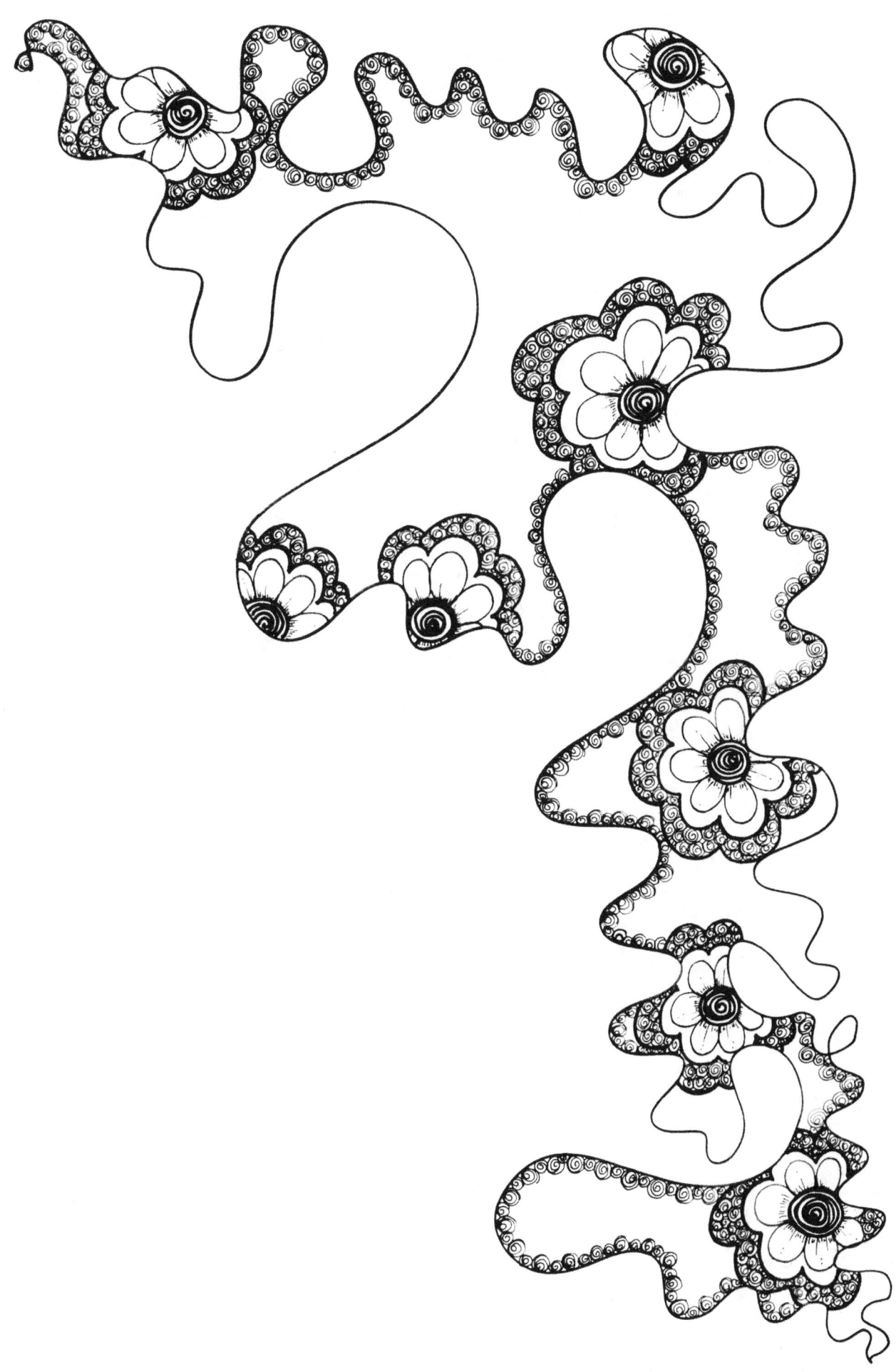

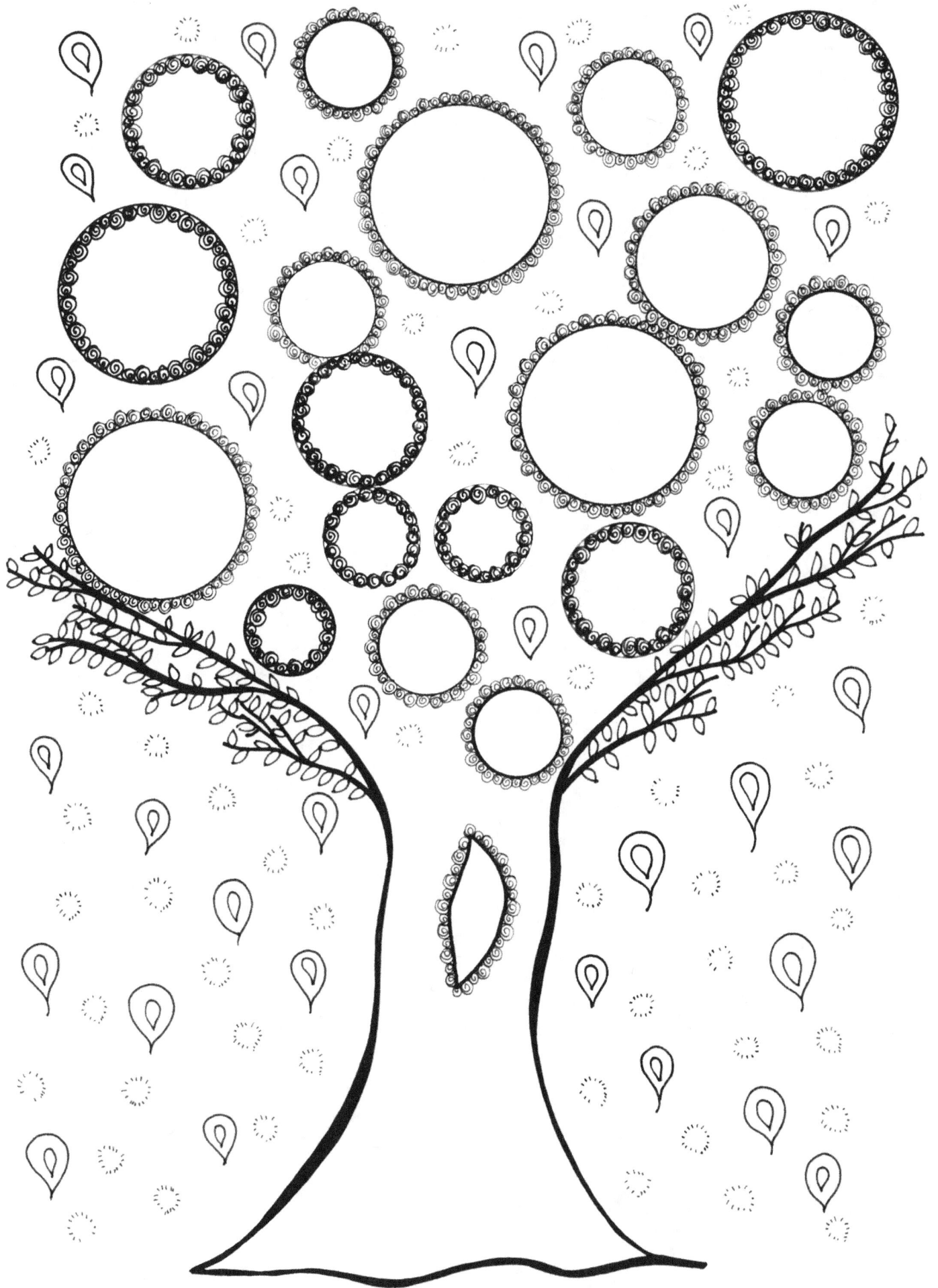

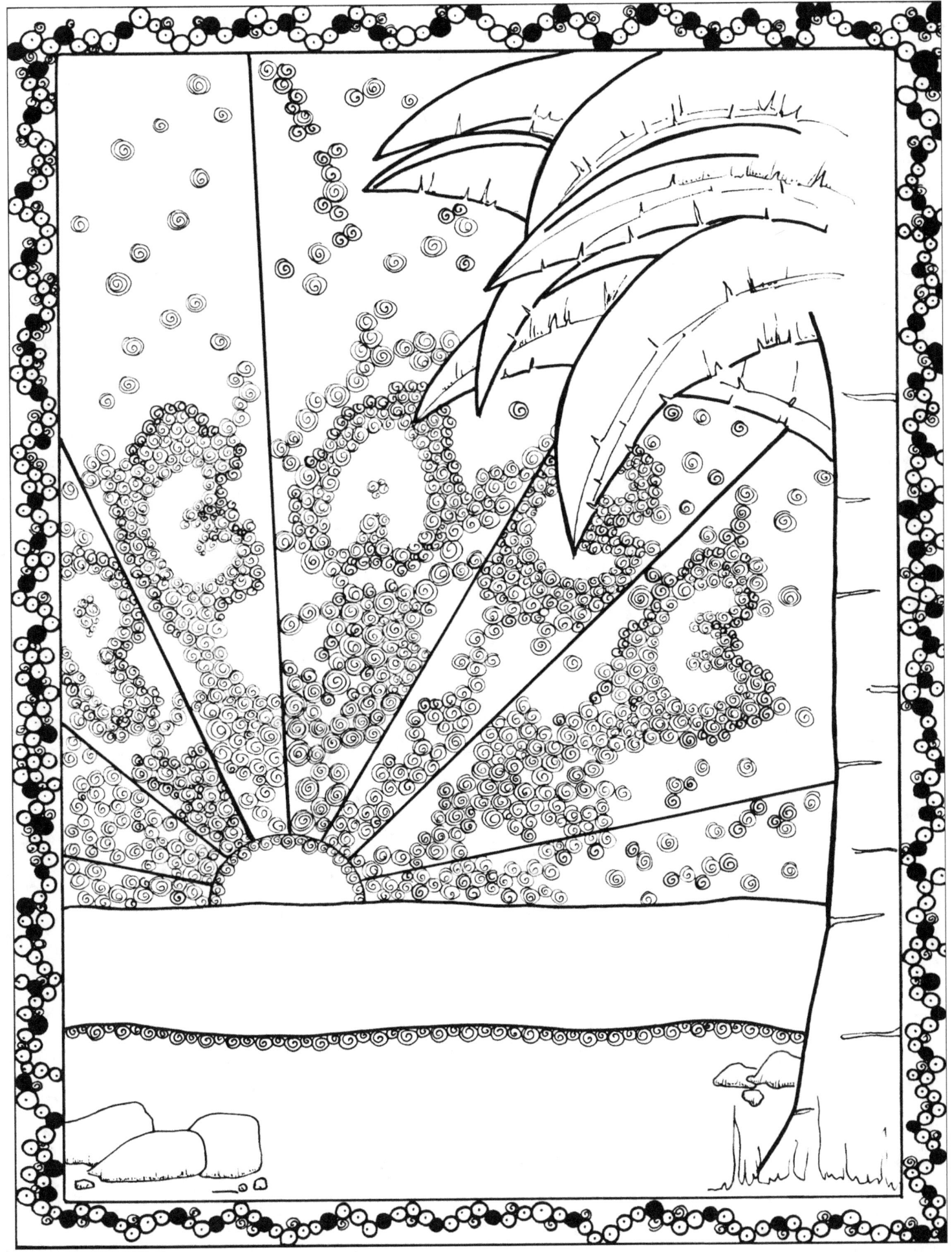

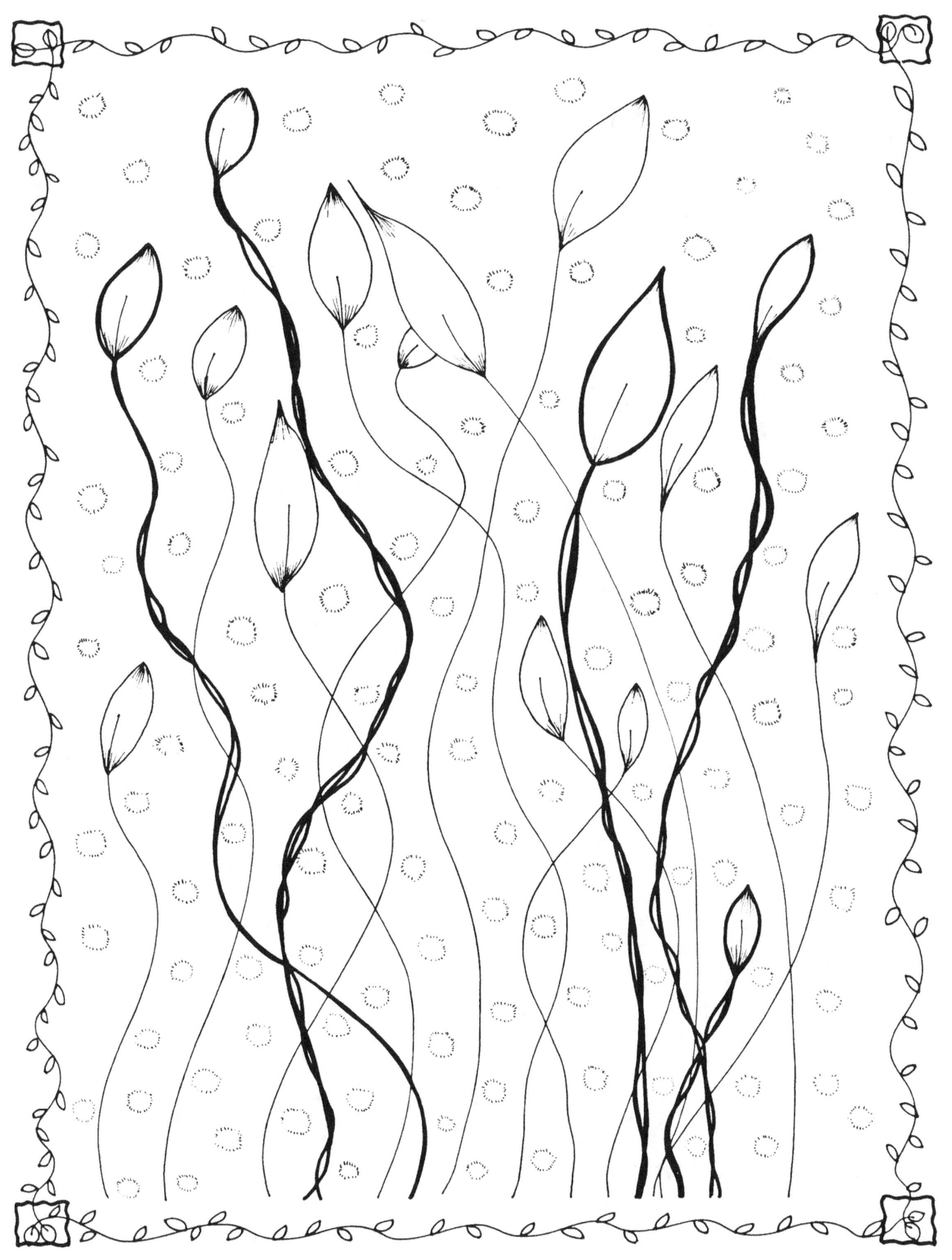

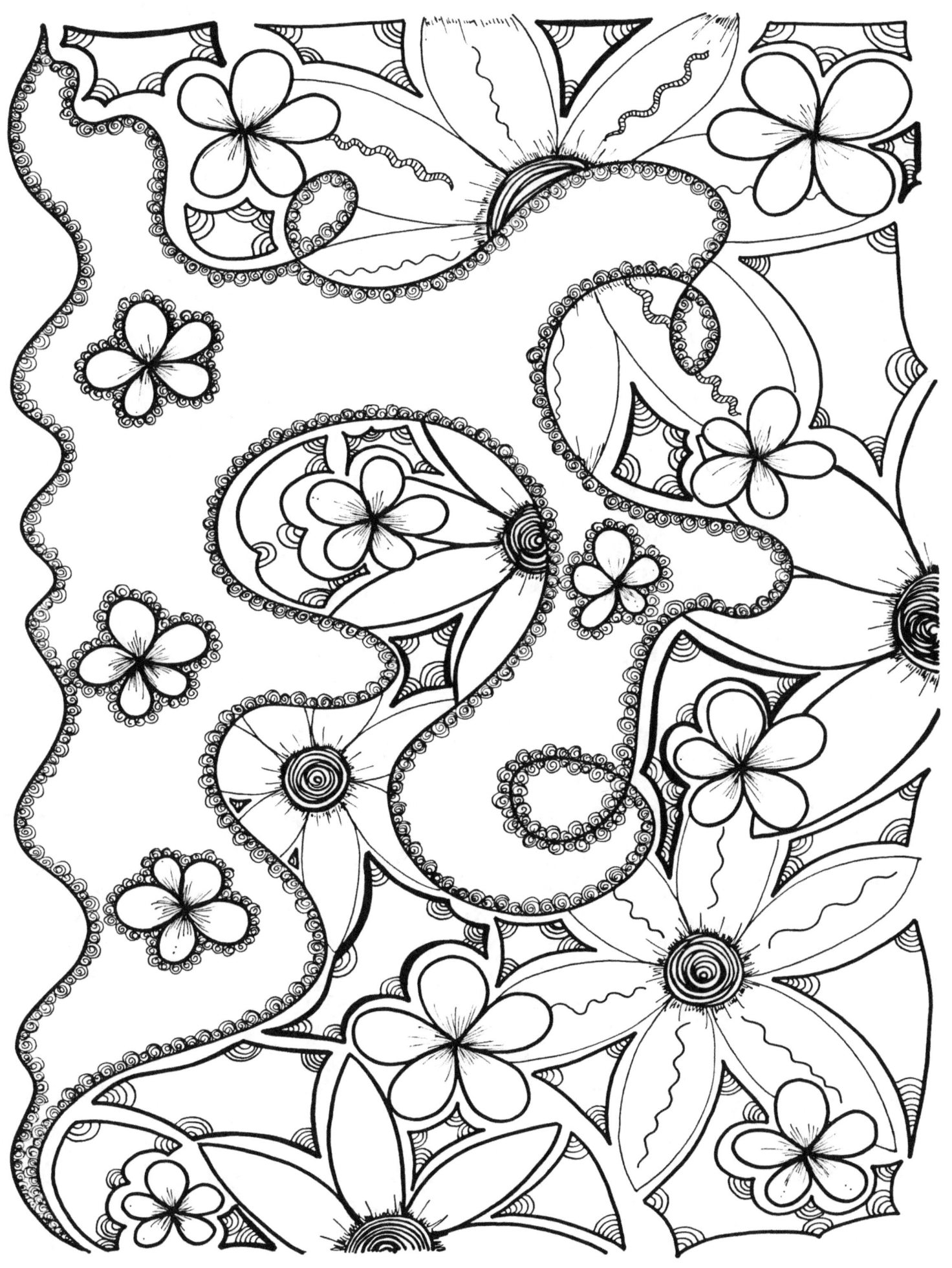

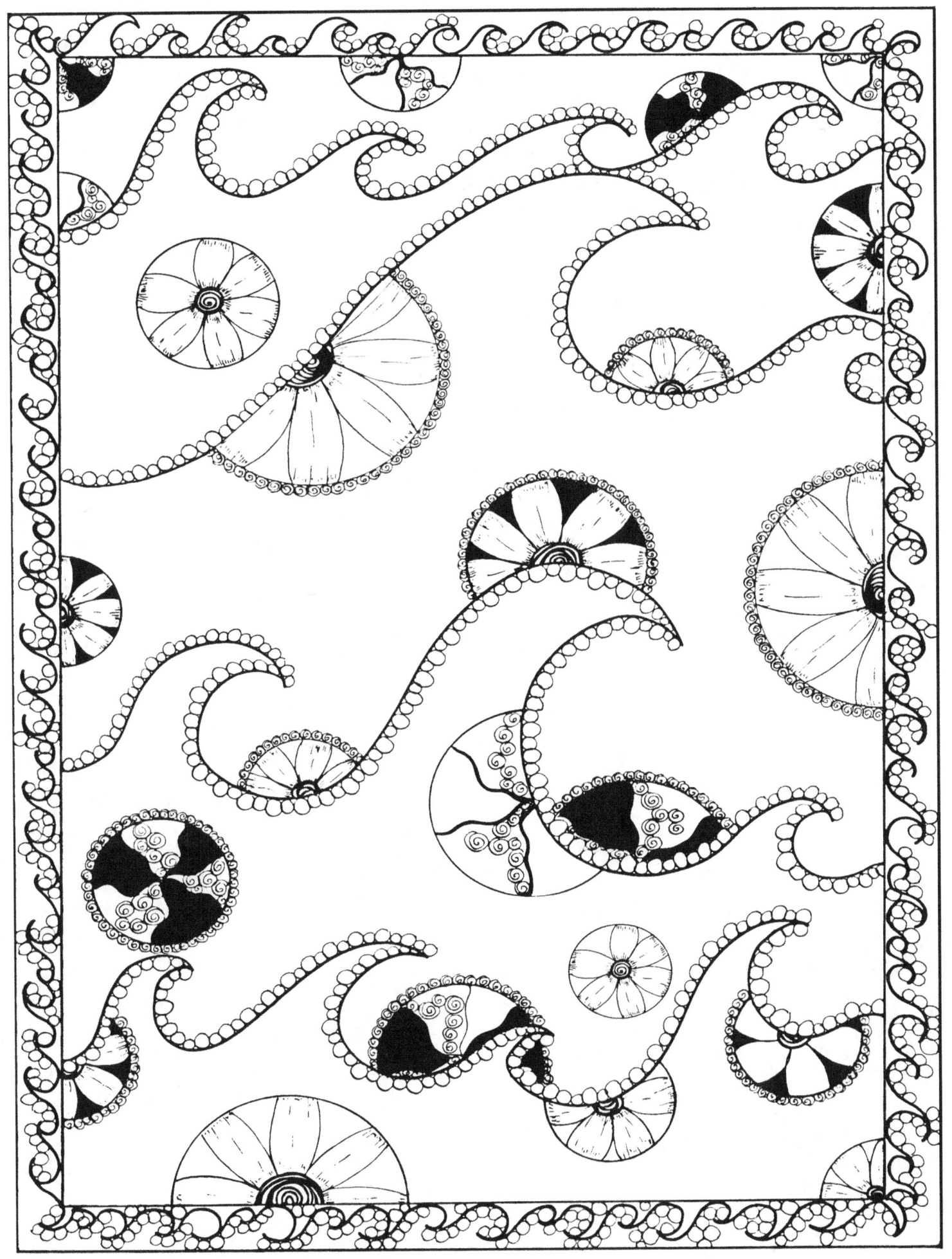

*Contributing Artist*
*L'aety Esperanza*
*France*

Facebook : Laety-Esperanza

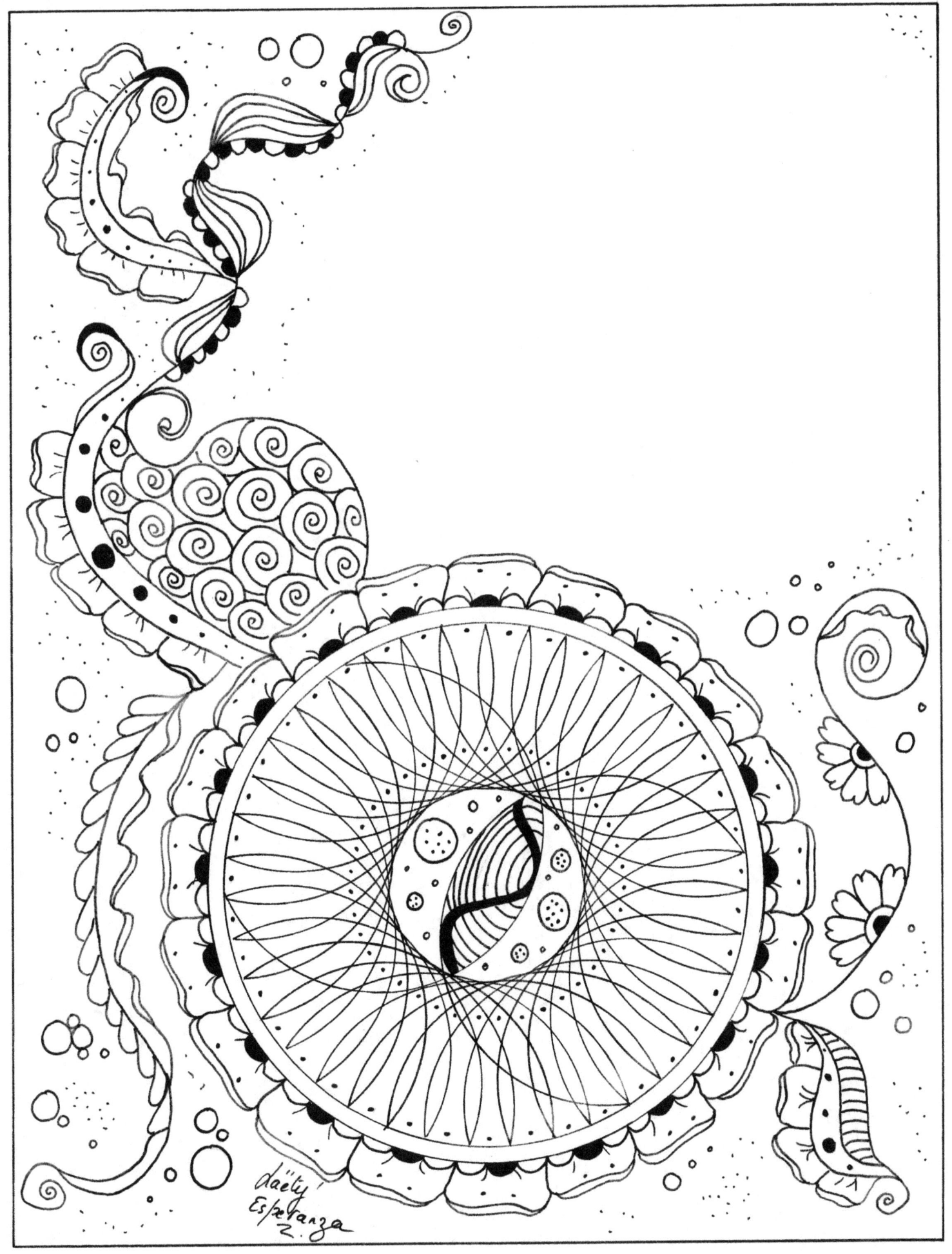

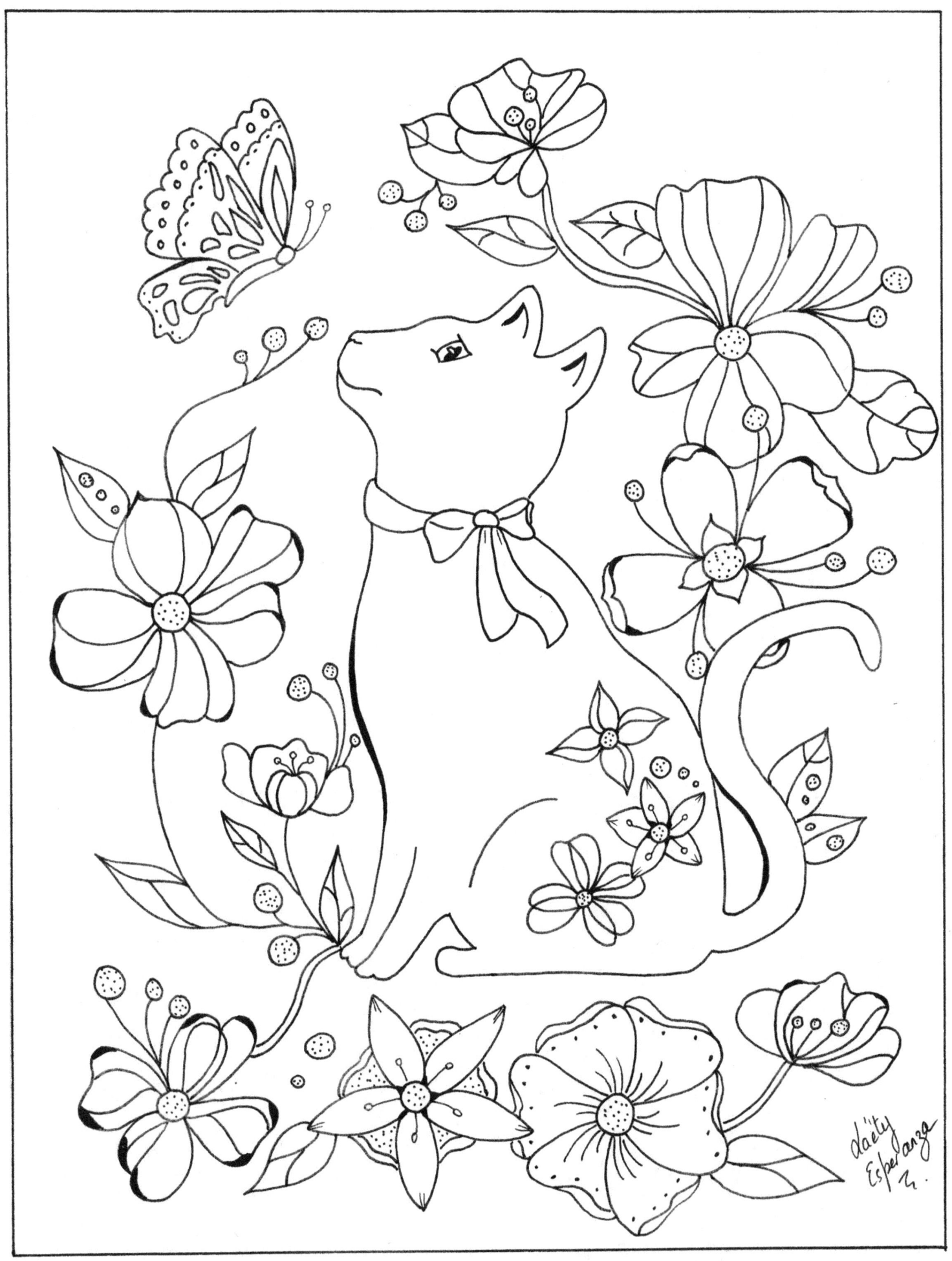

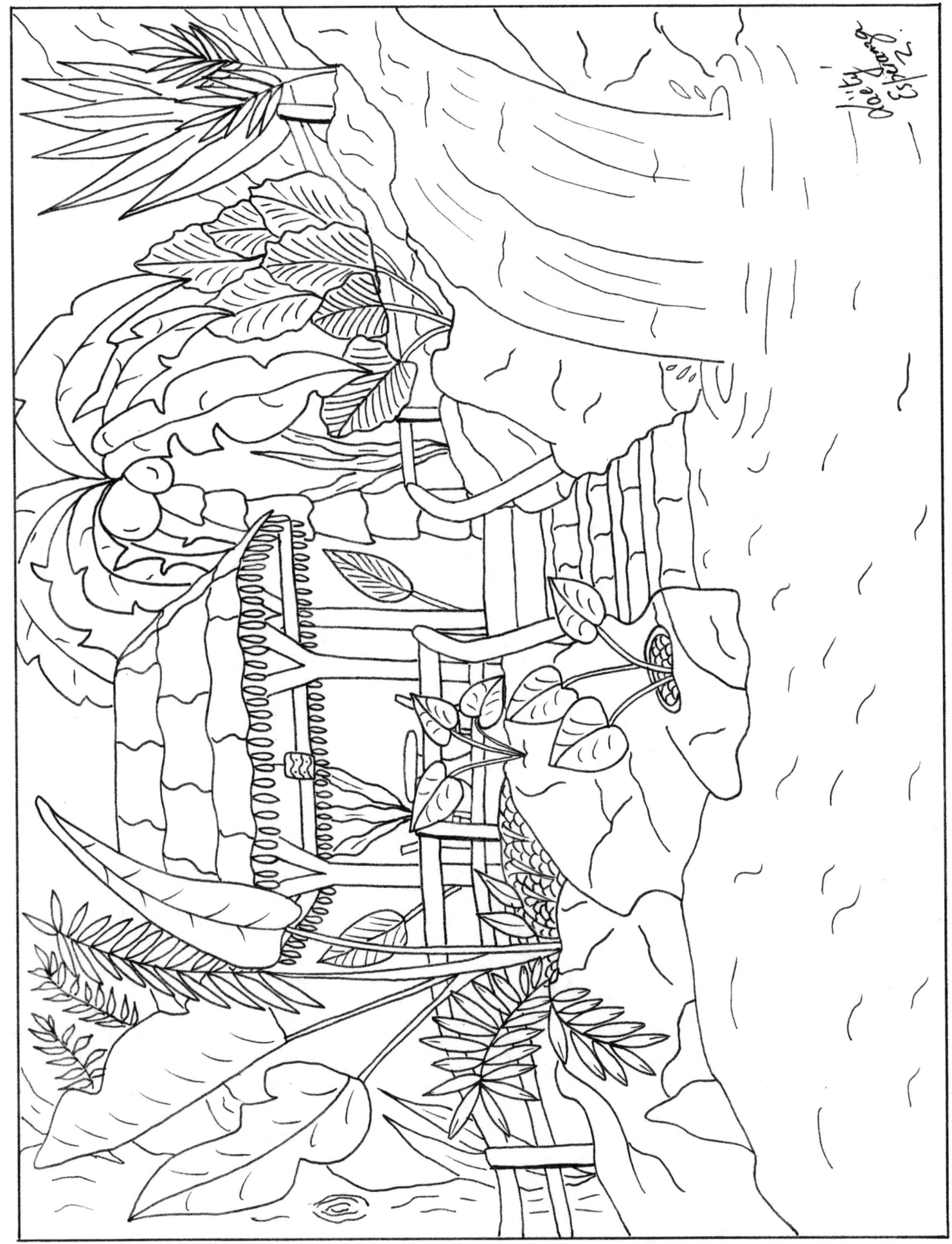

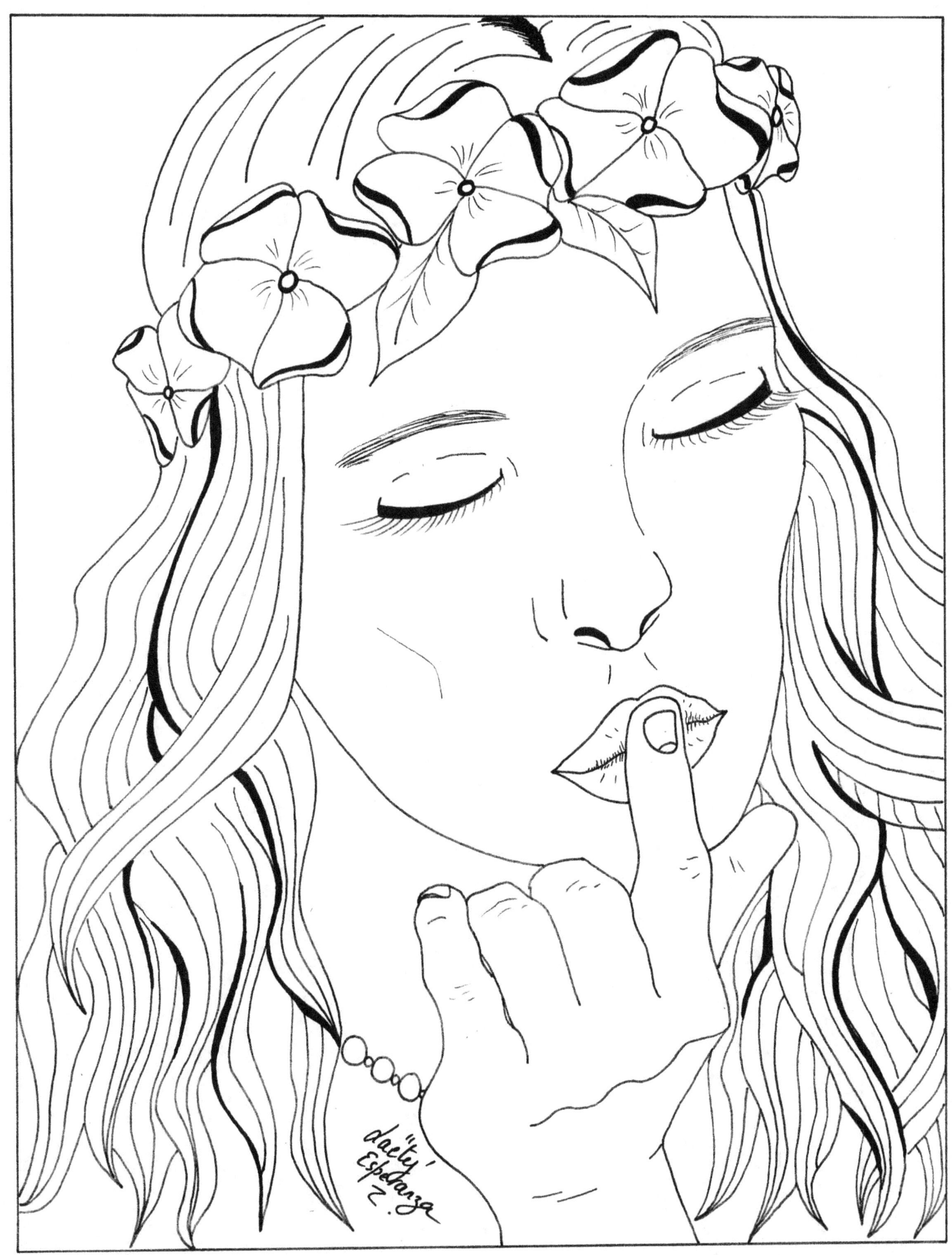

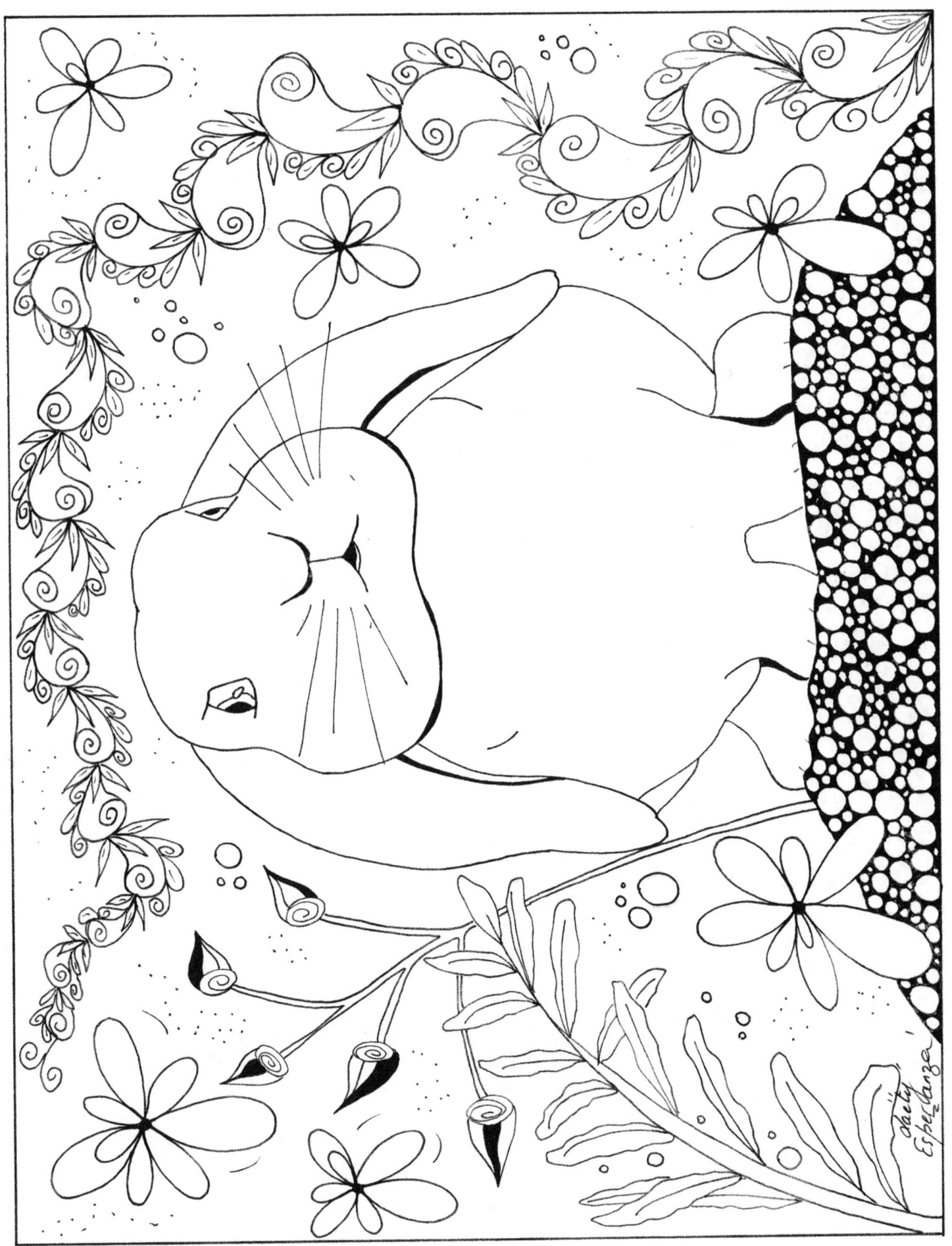

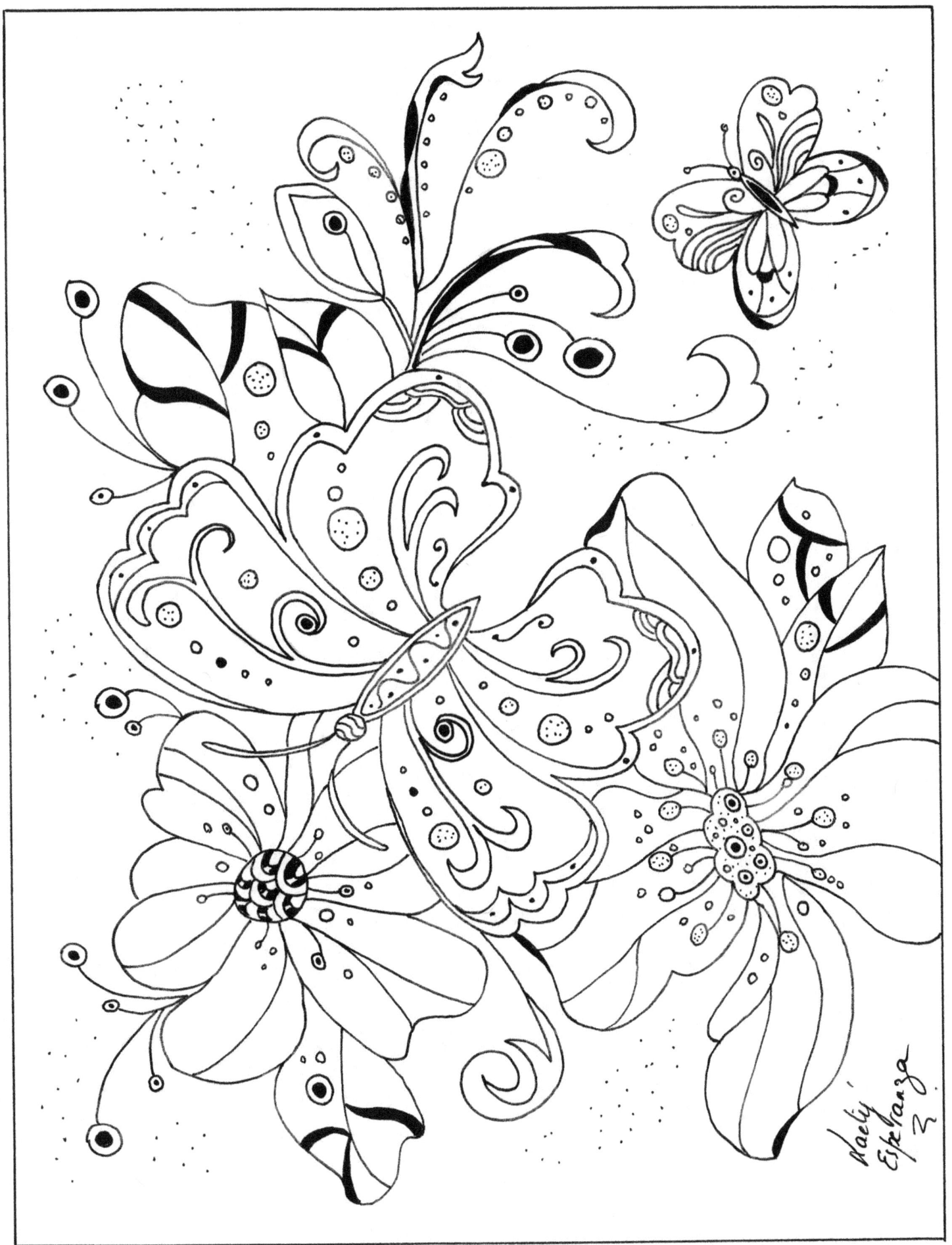

*Contributing Artist*
*Alison Civil*
*USA*

Facebook : alisoncivilart

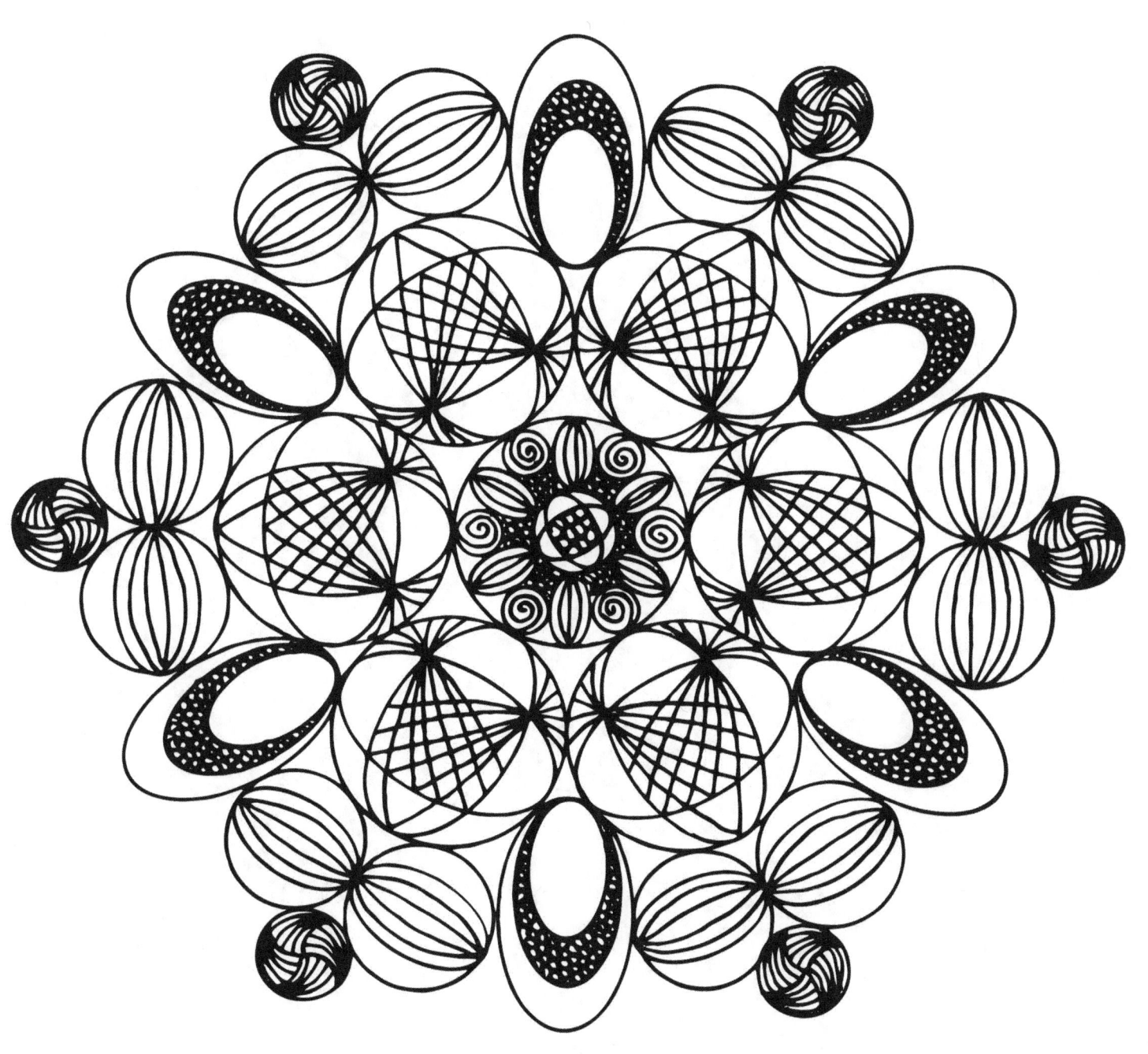

AJC Aug 2015

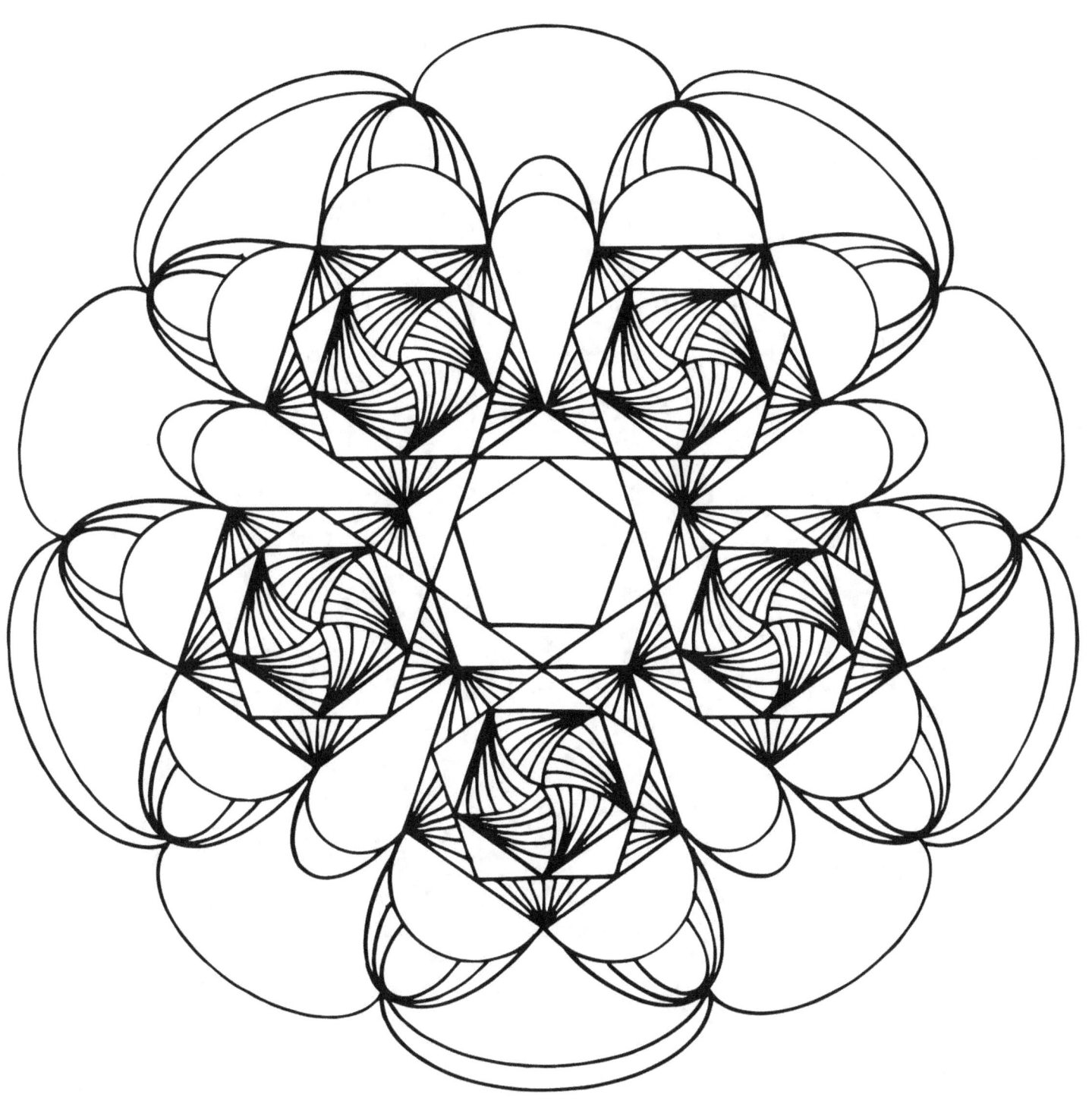

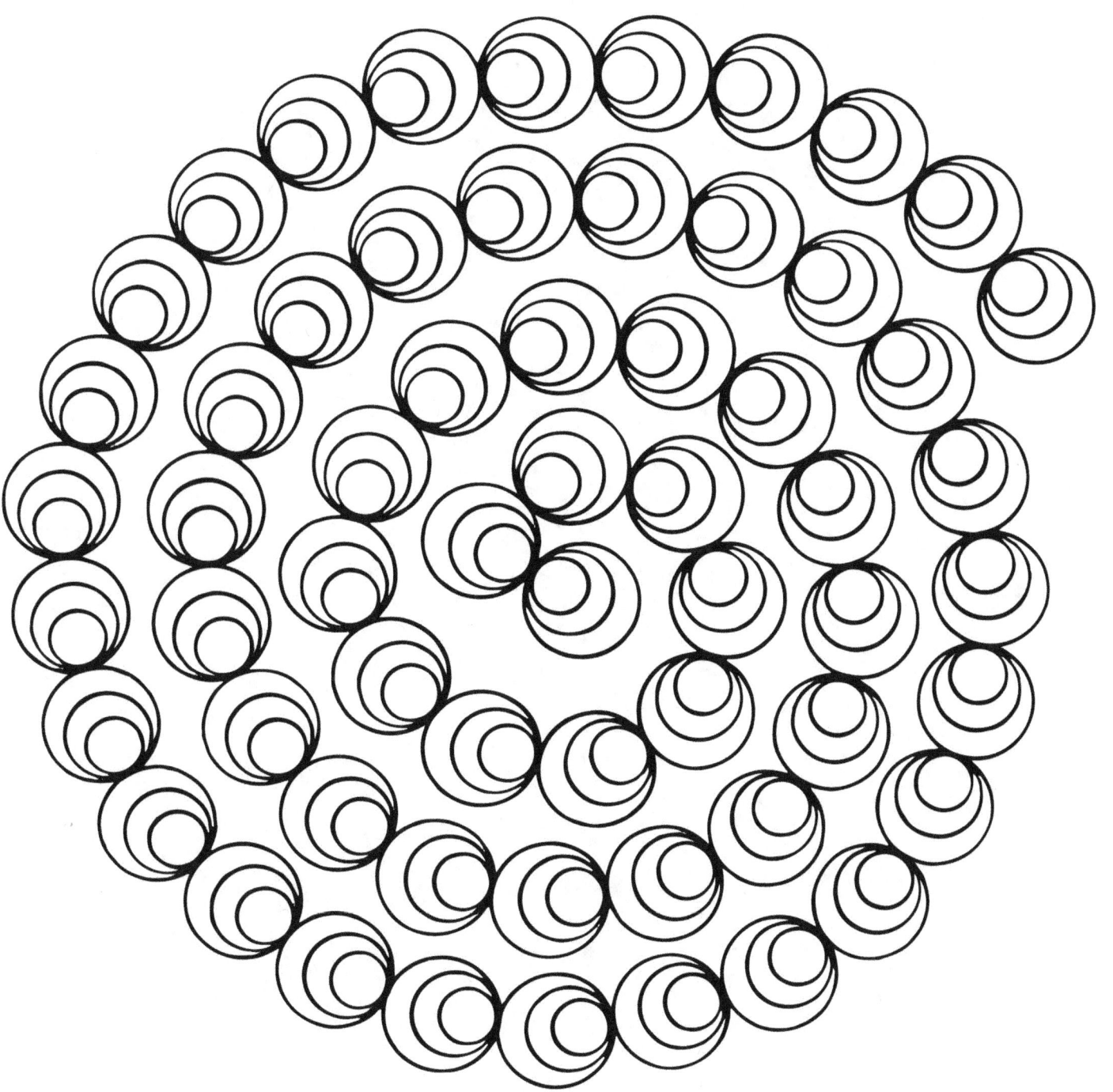

AJC Sept 2015

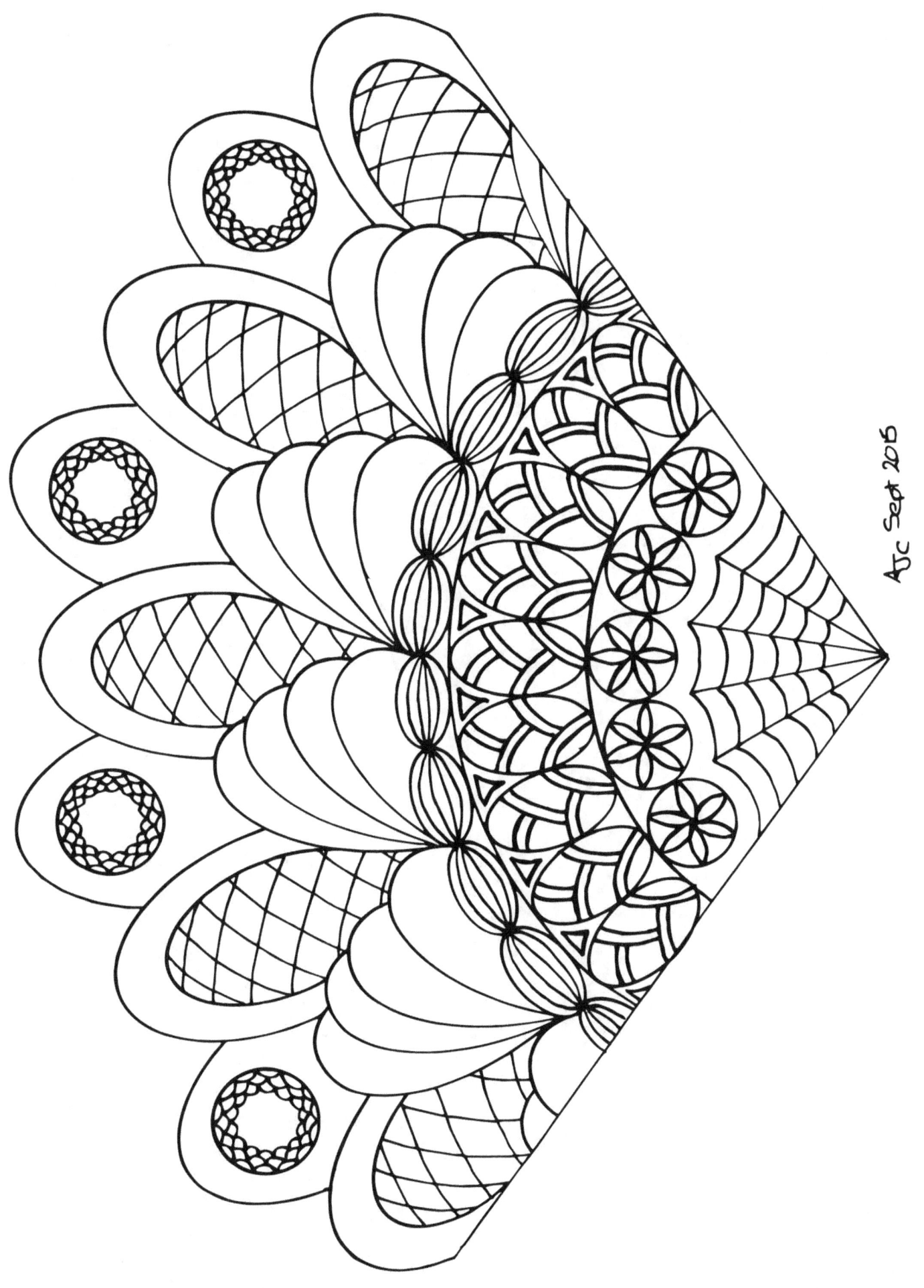

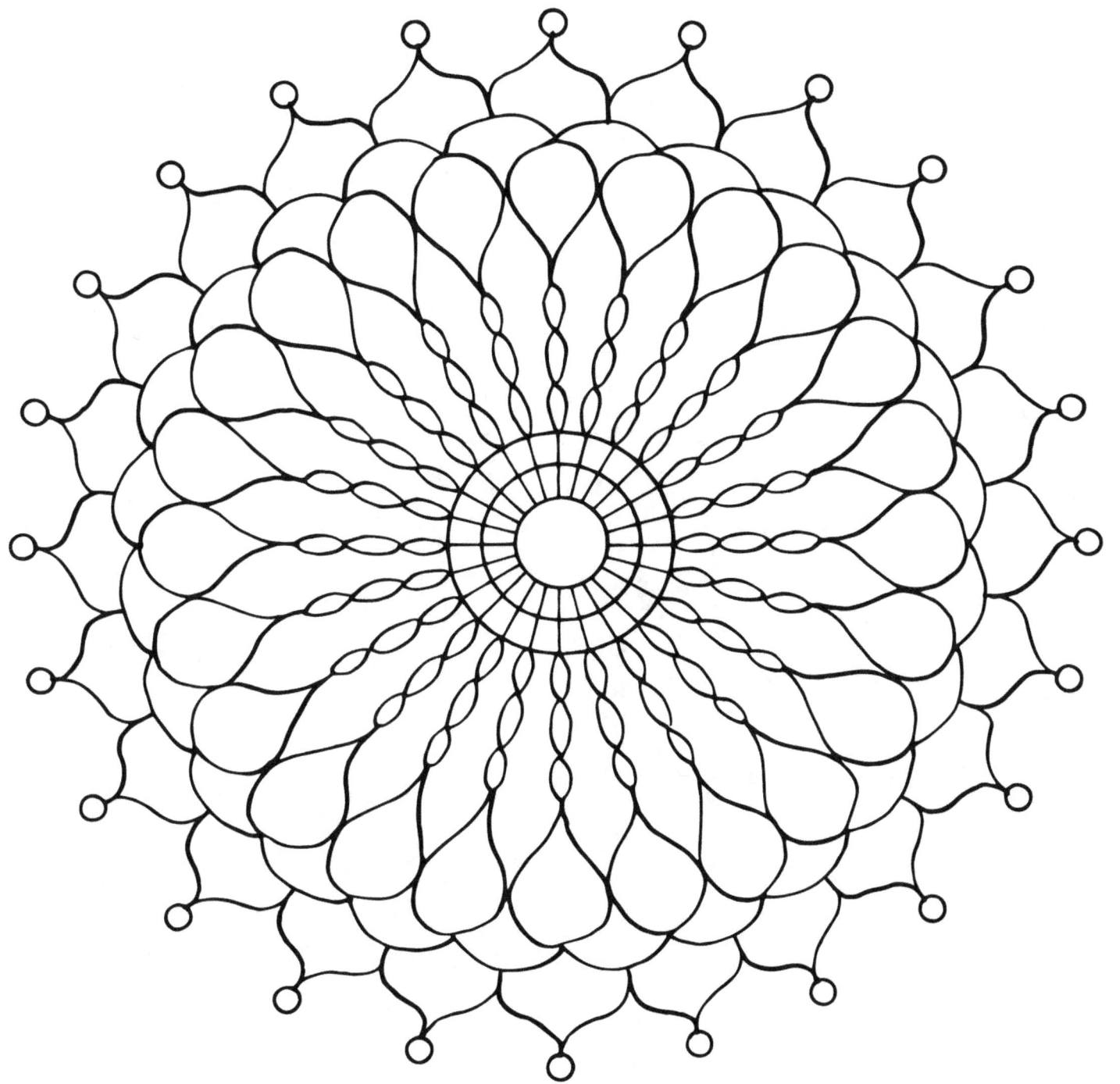

AJC Sept 2015

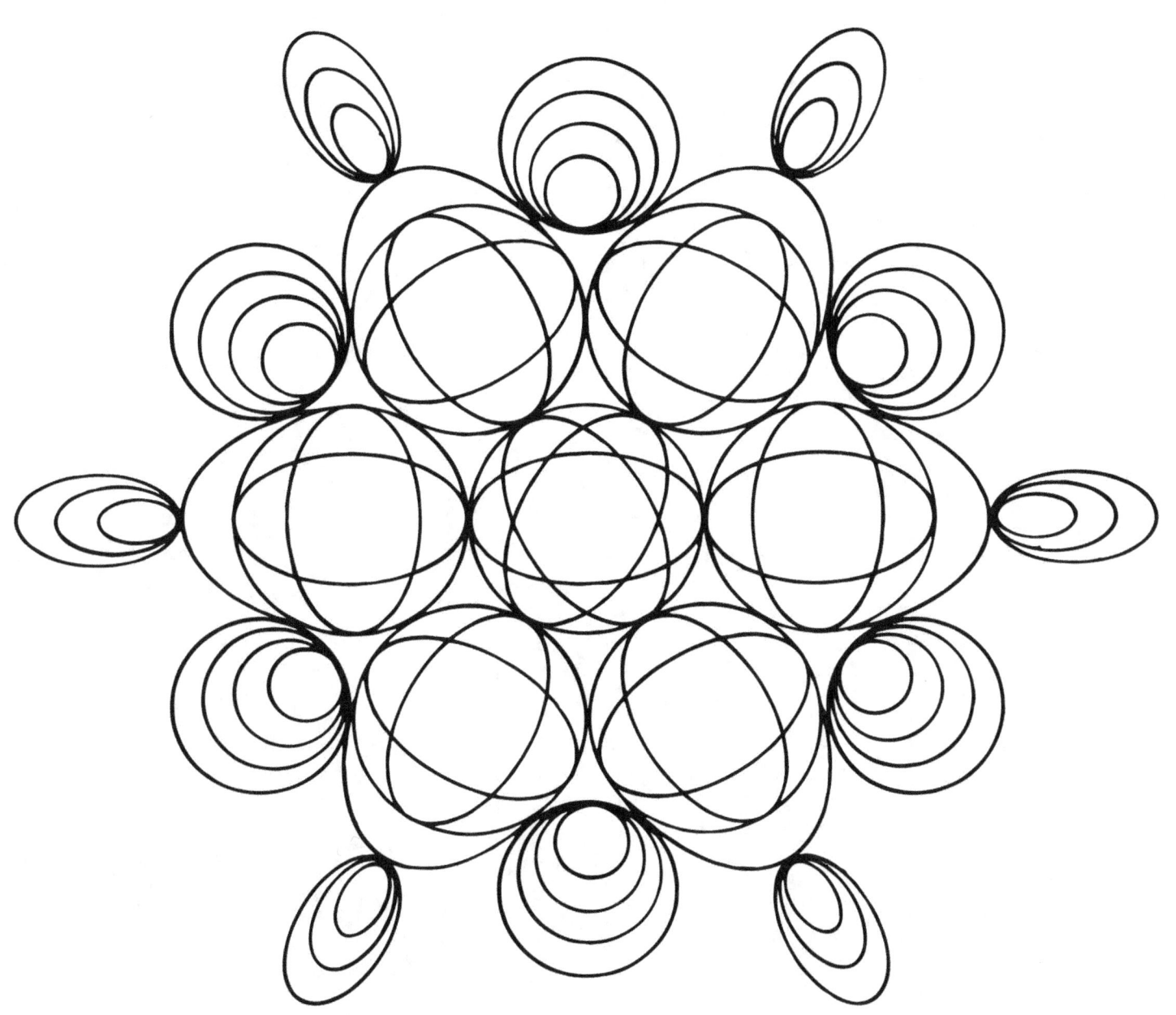

AJC Sept 2015

*Contributing Artist*
*Jodi Ho*
*Taiwan*

Facebook : Dream jodi's dream

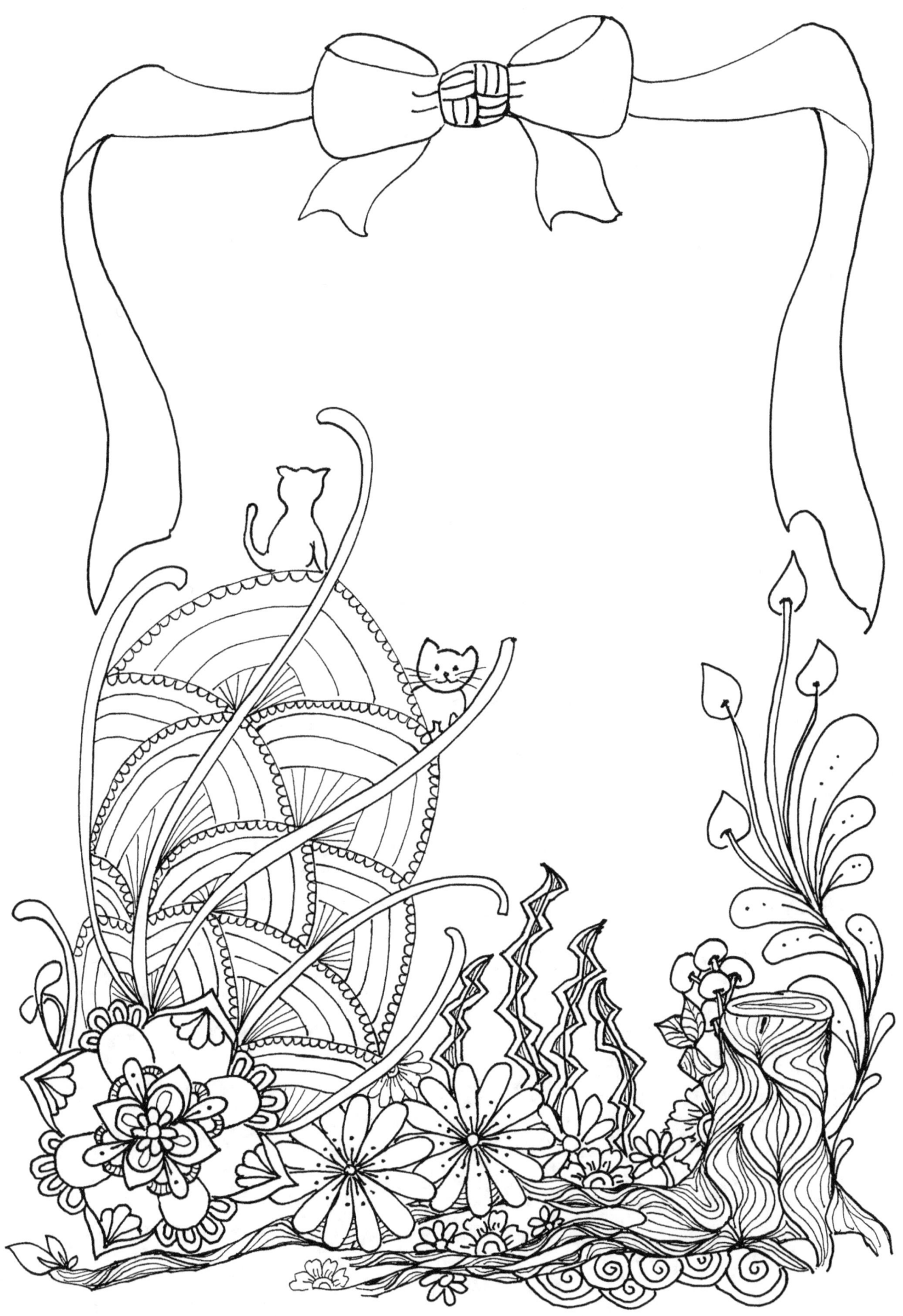

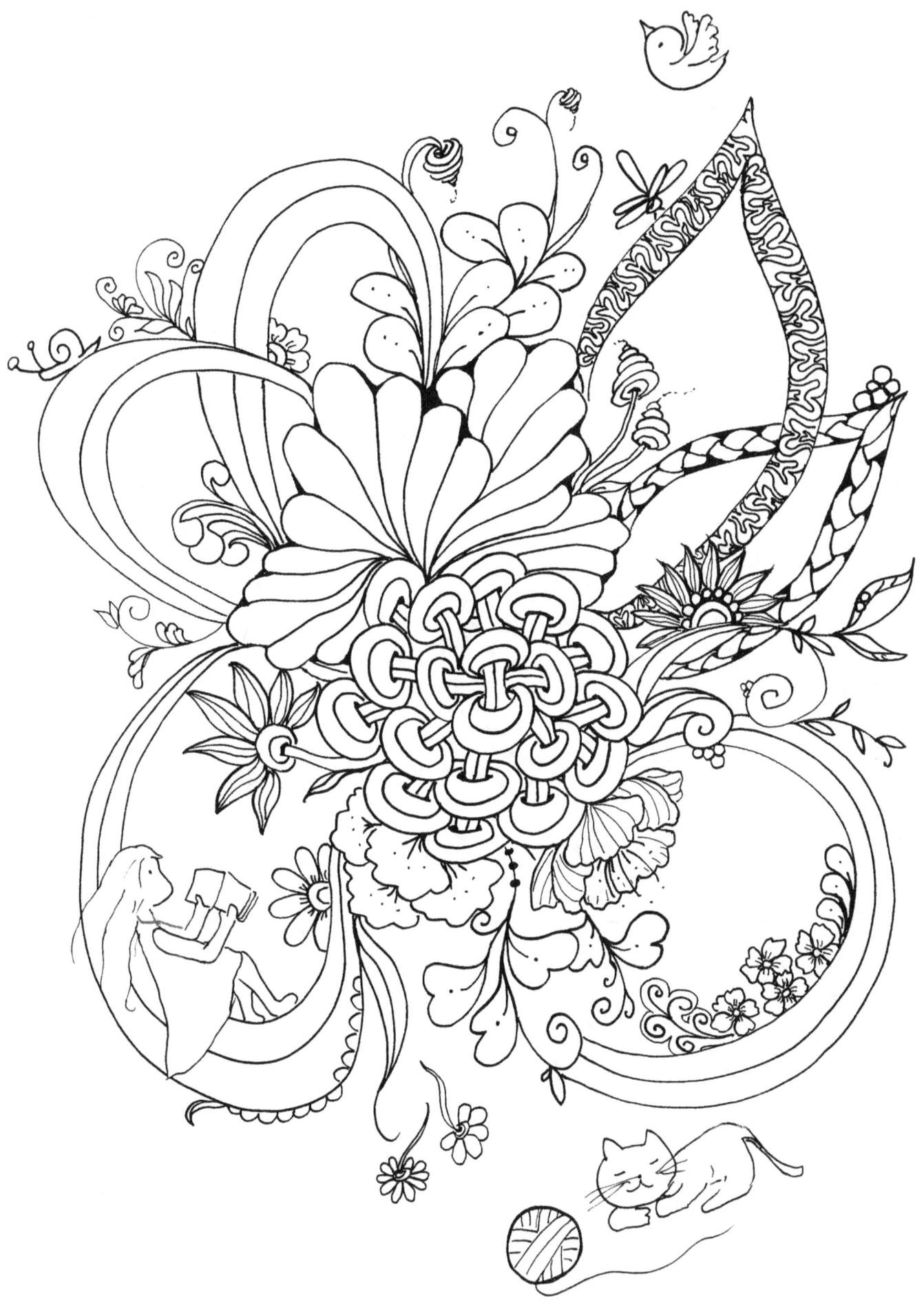

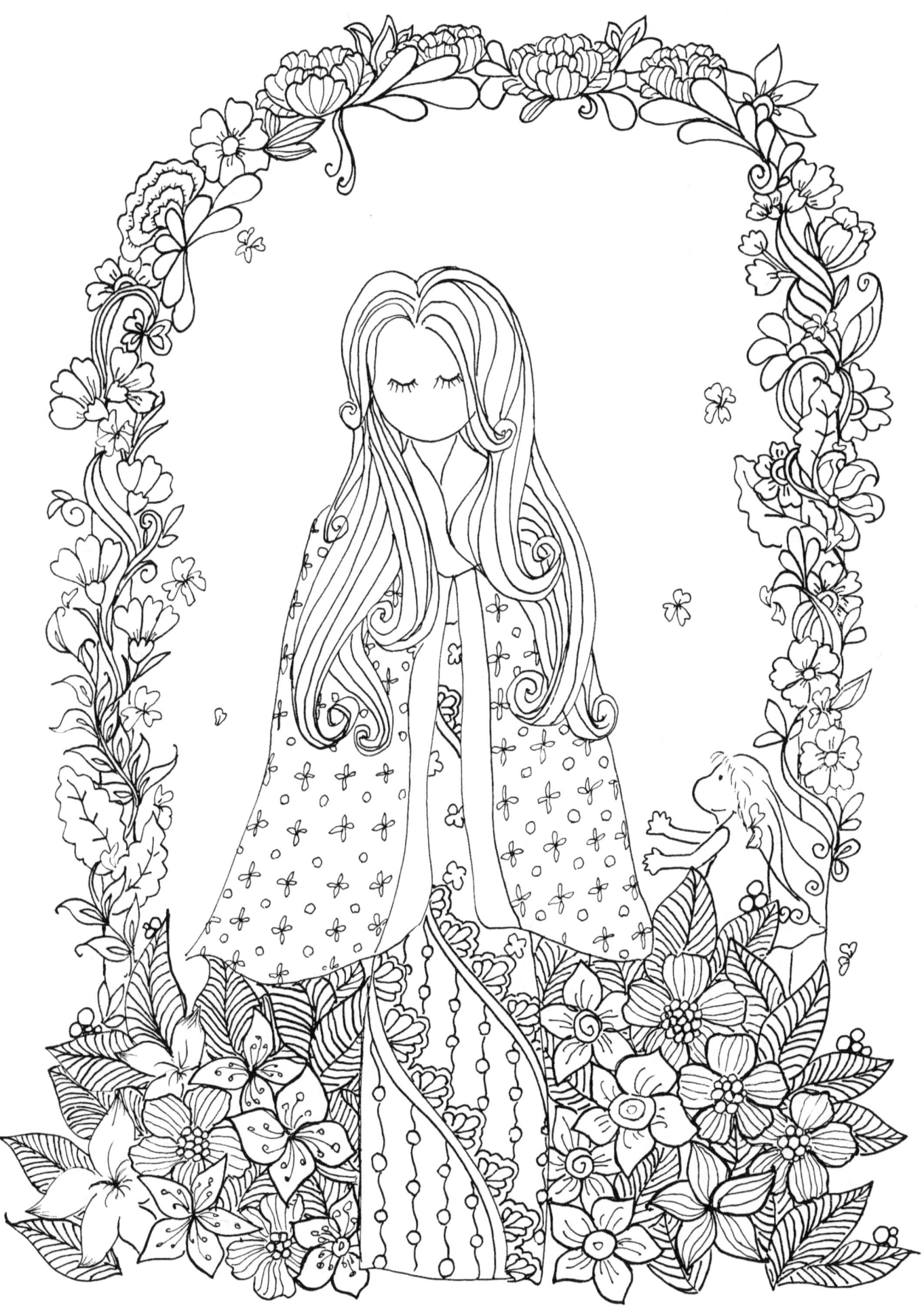

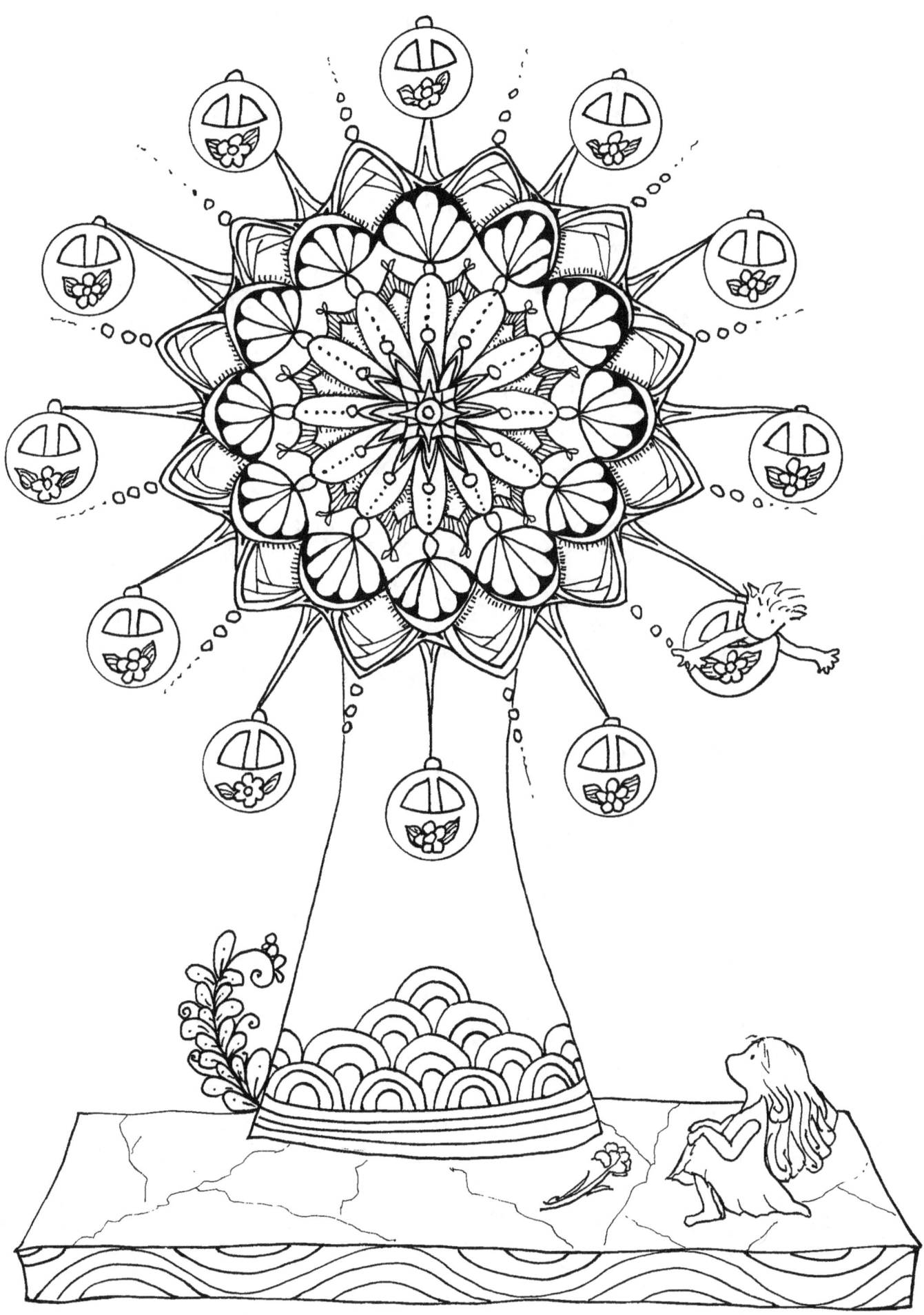

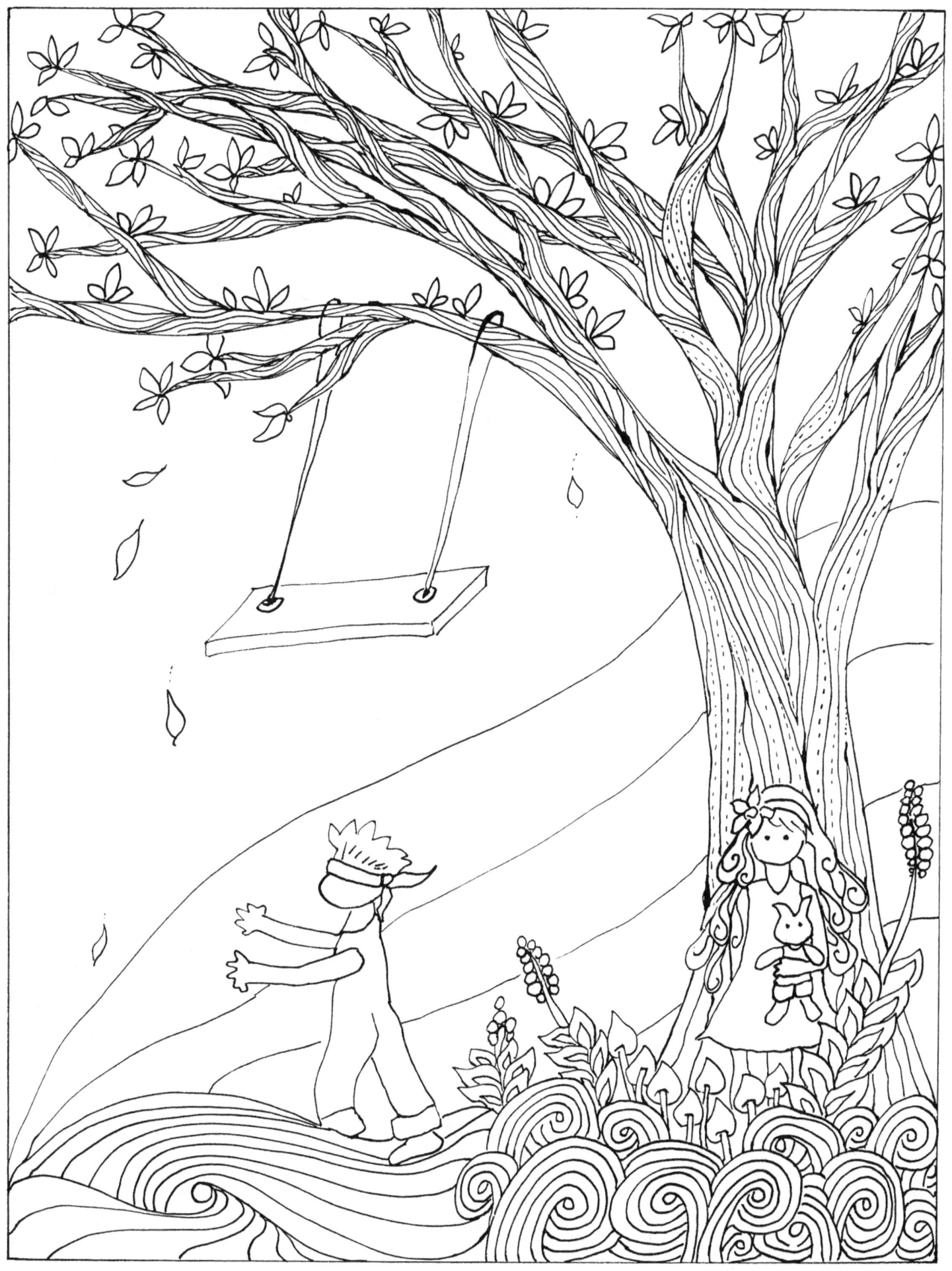

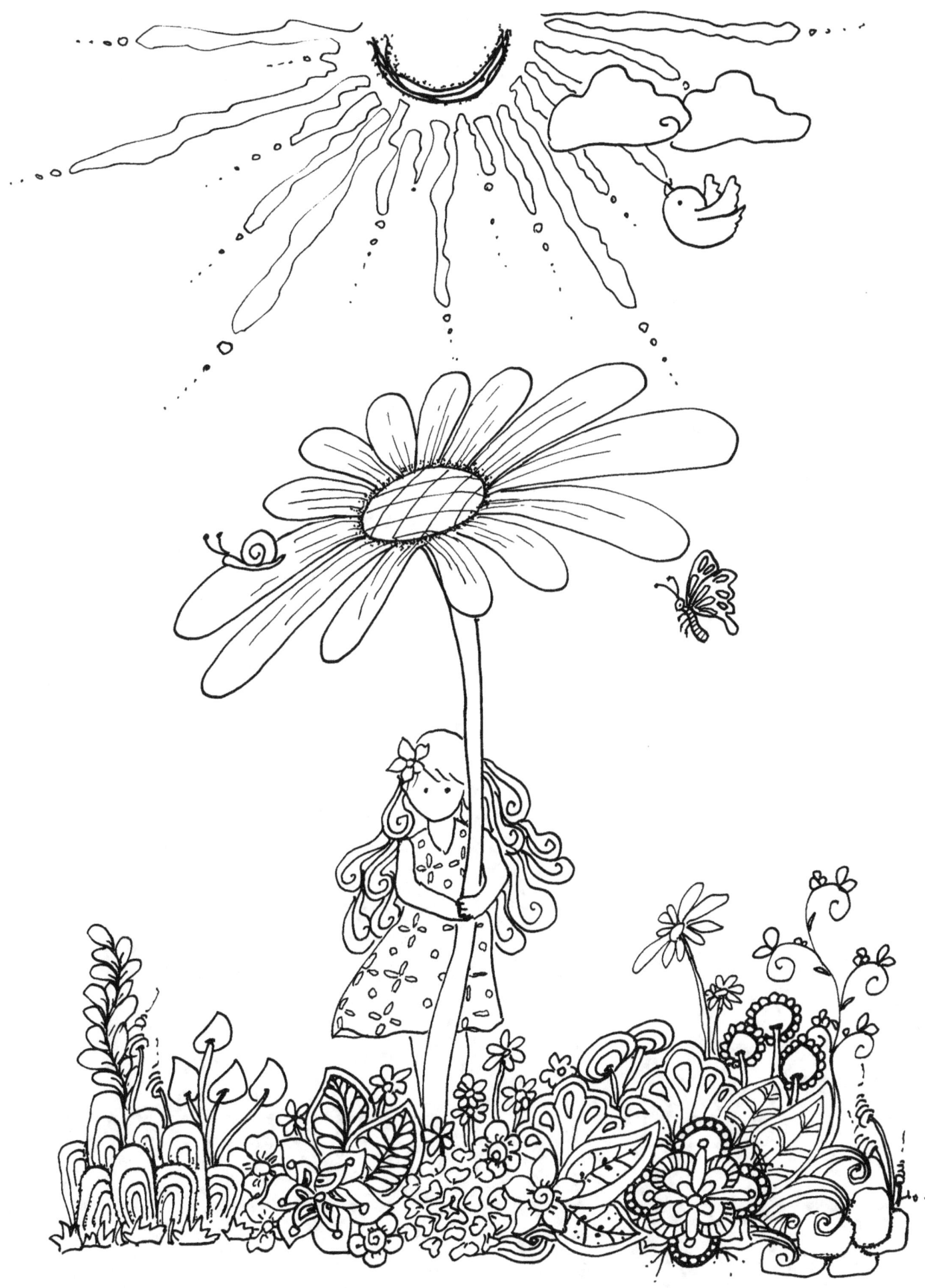

*Contributing Artist*
*Judy West*
*USA*

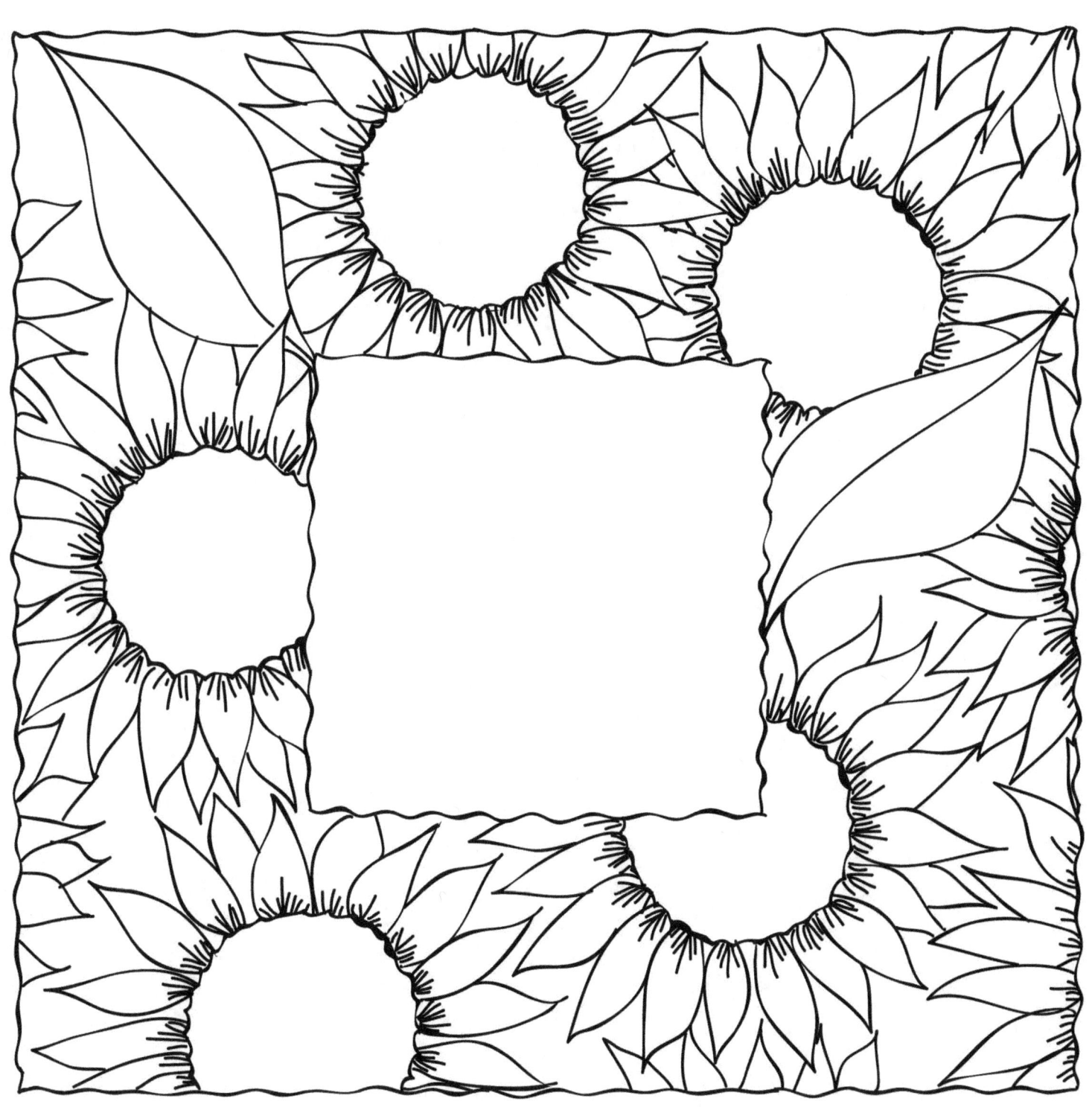

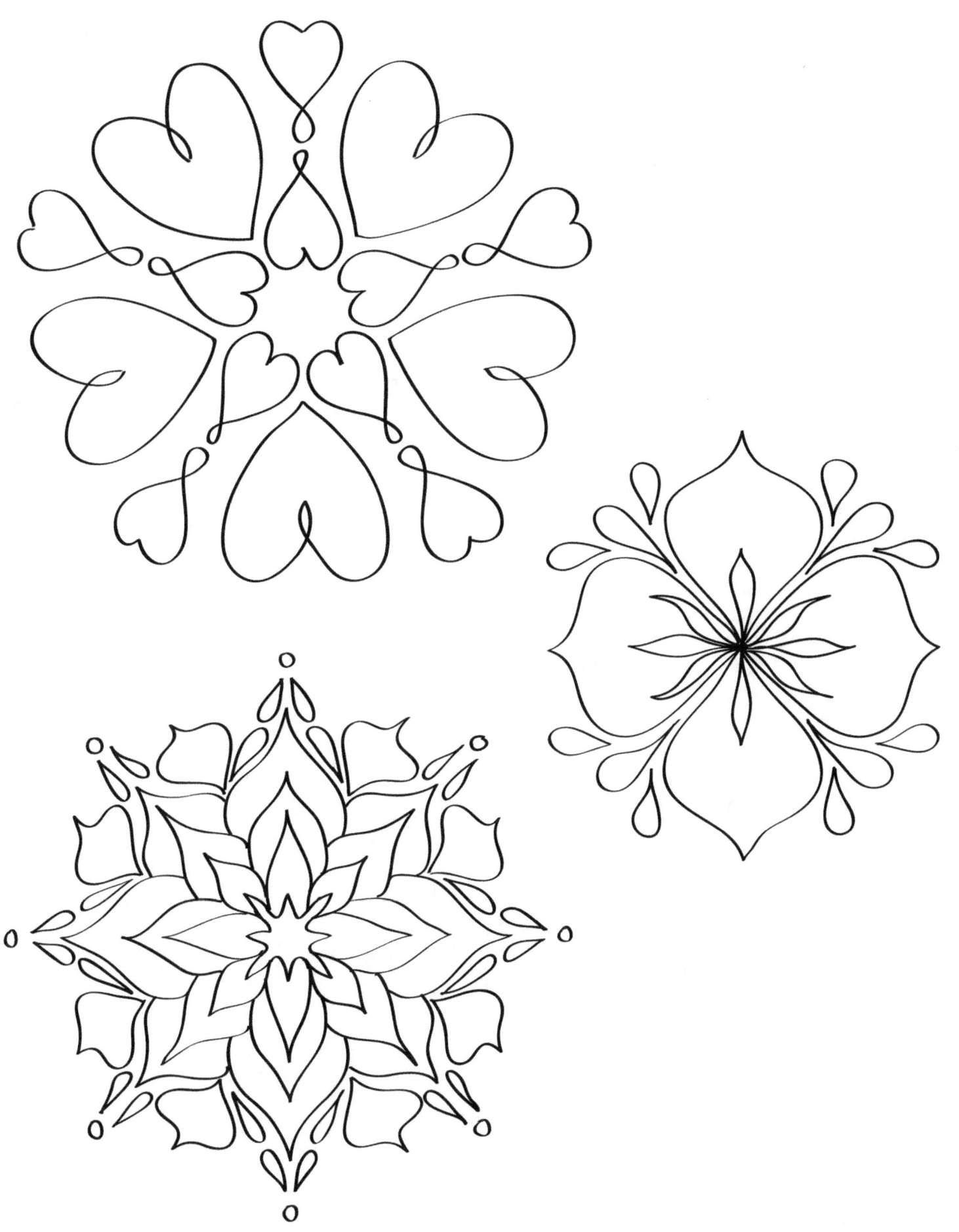

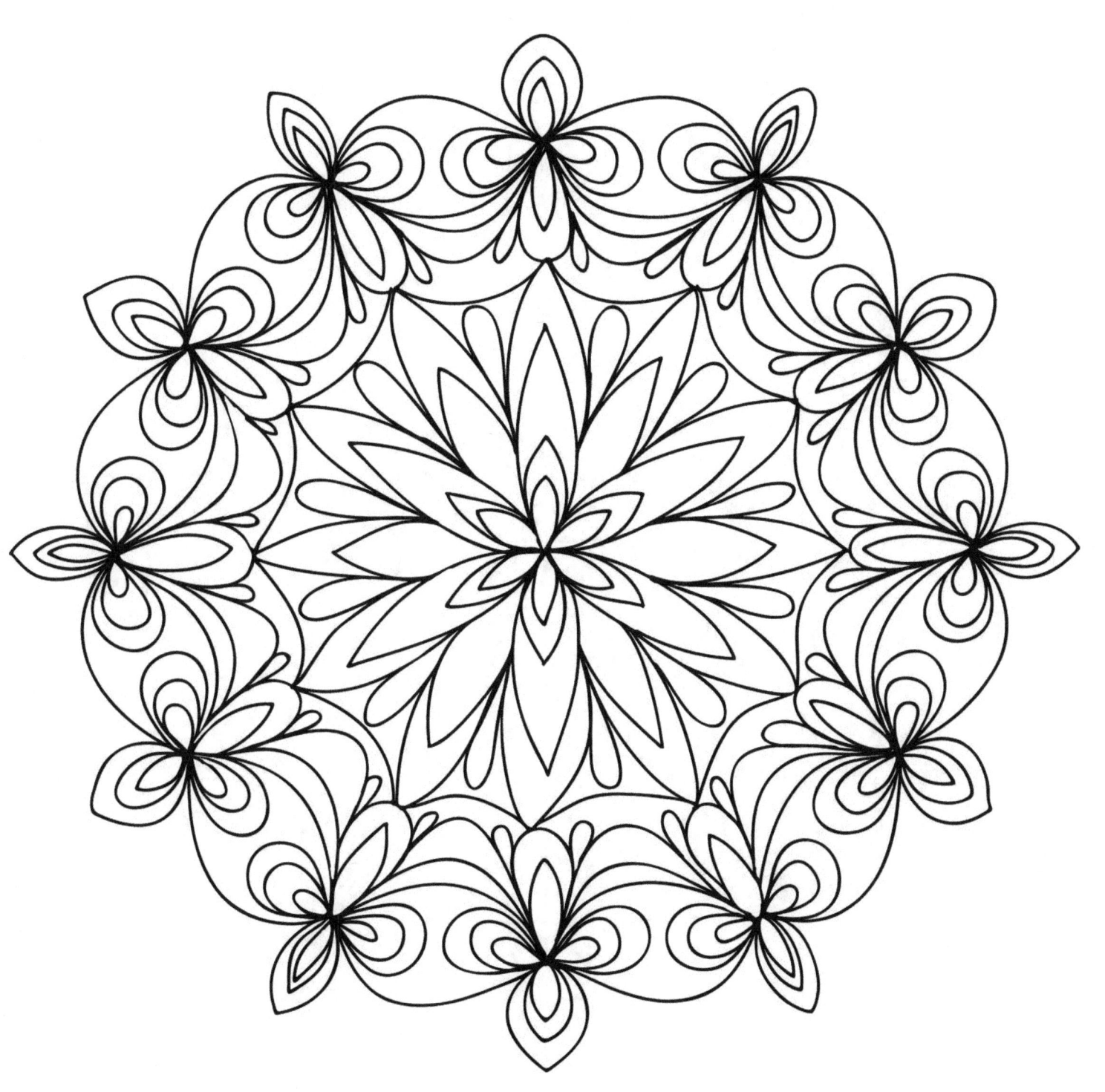

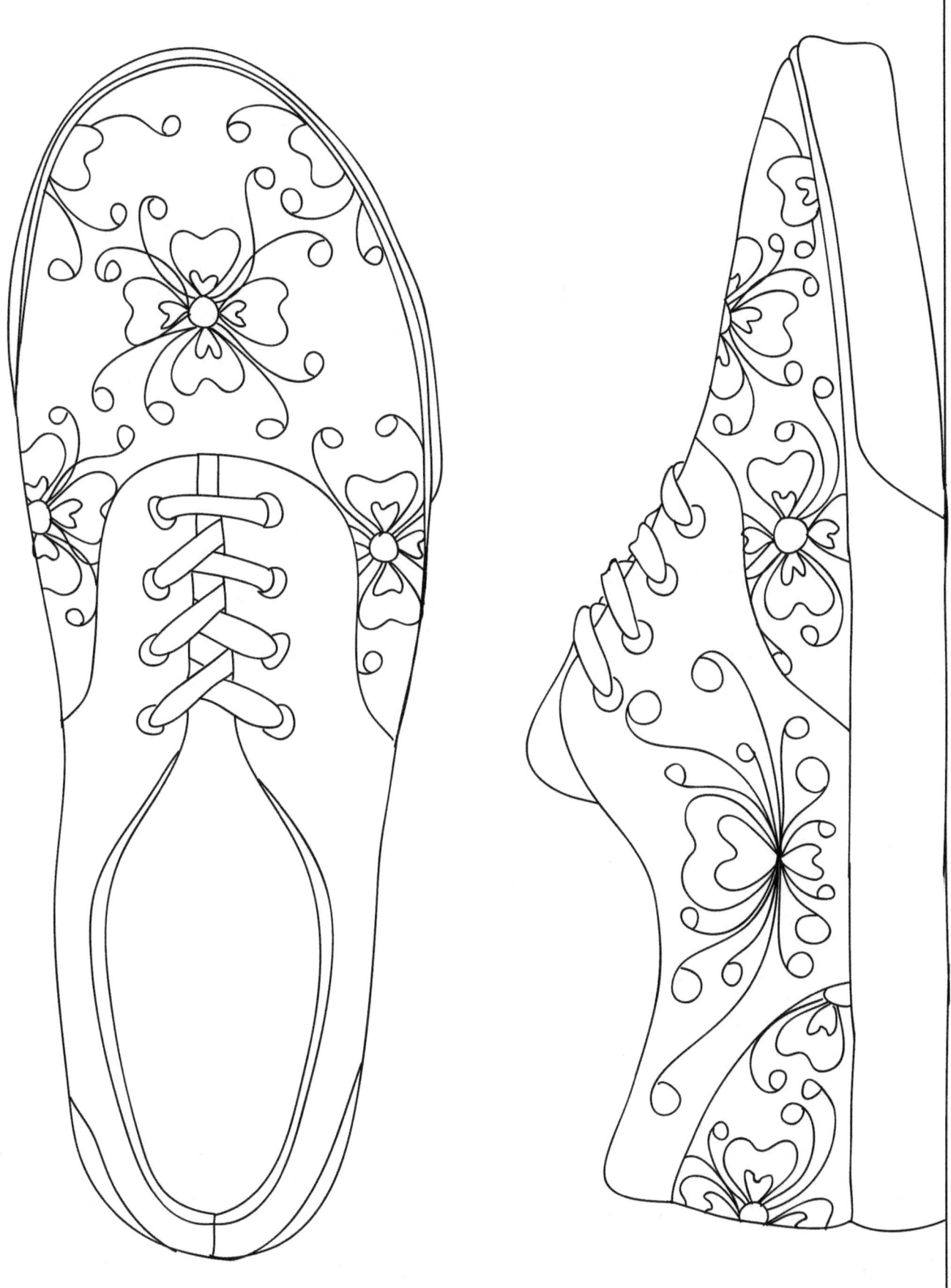

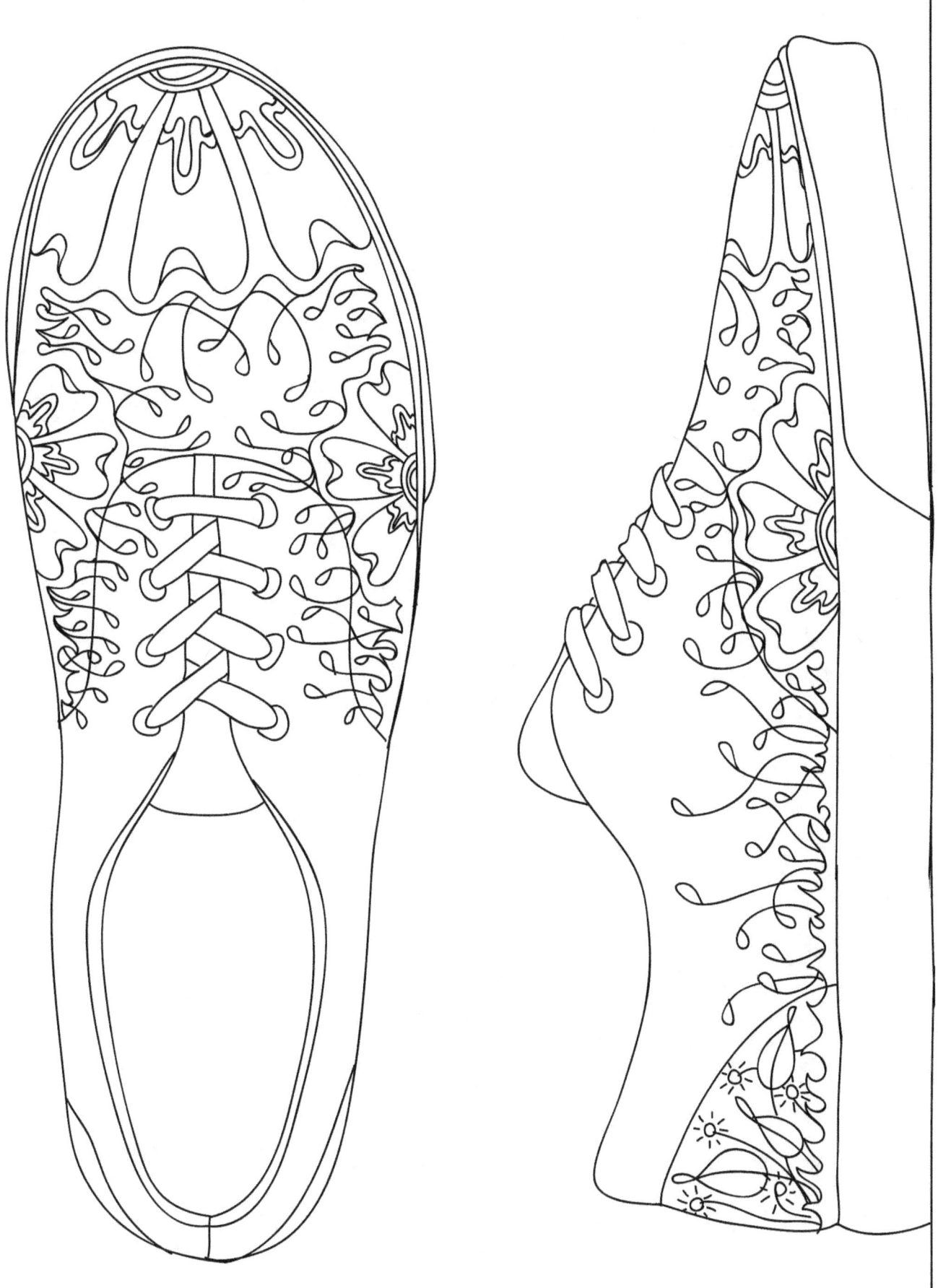

*Contributing Artist*
*Tamara A. Cameron*
*USA*

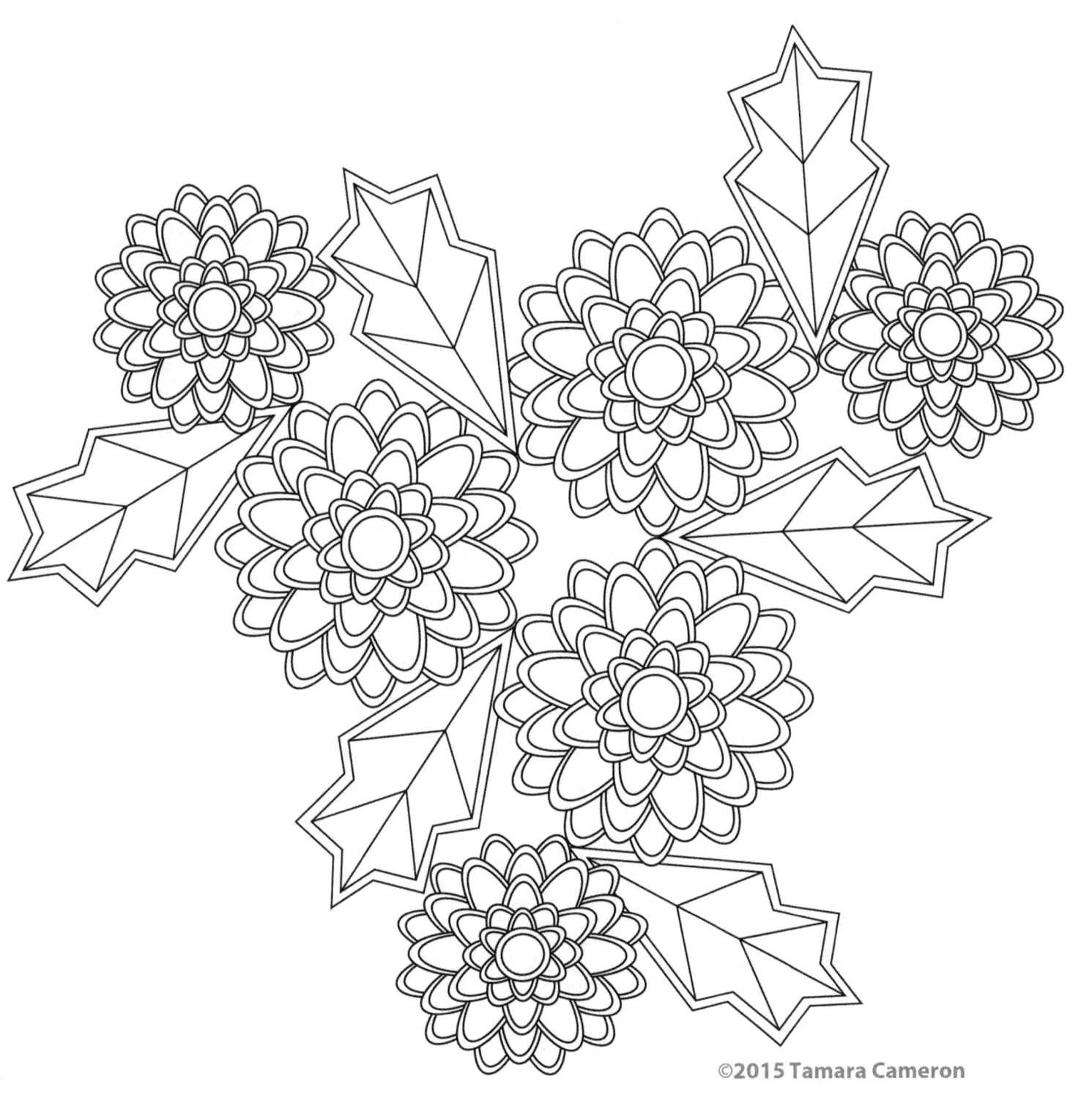

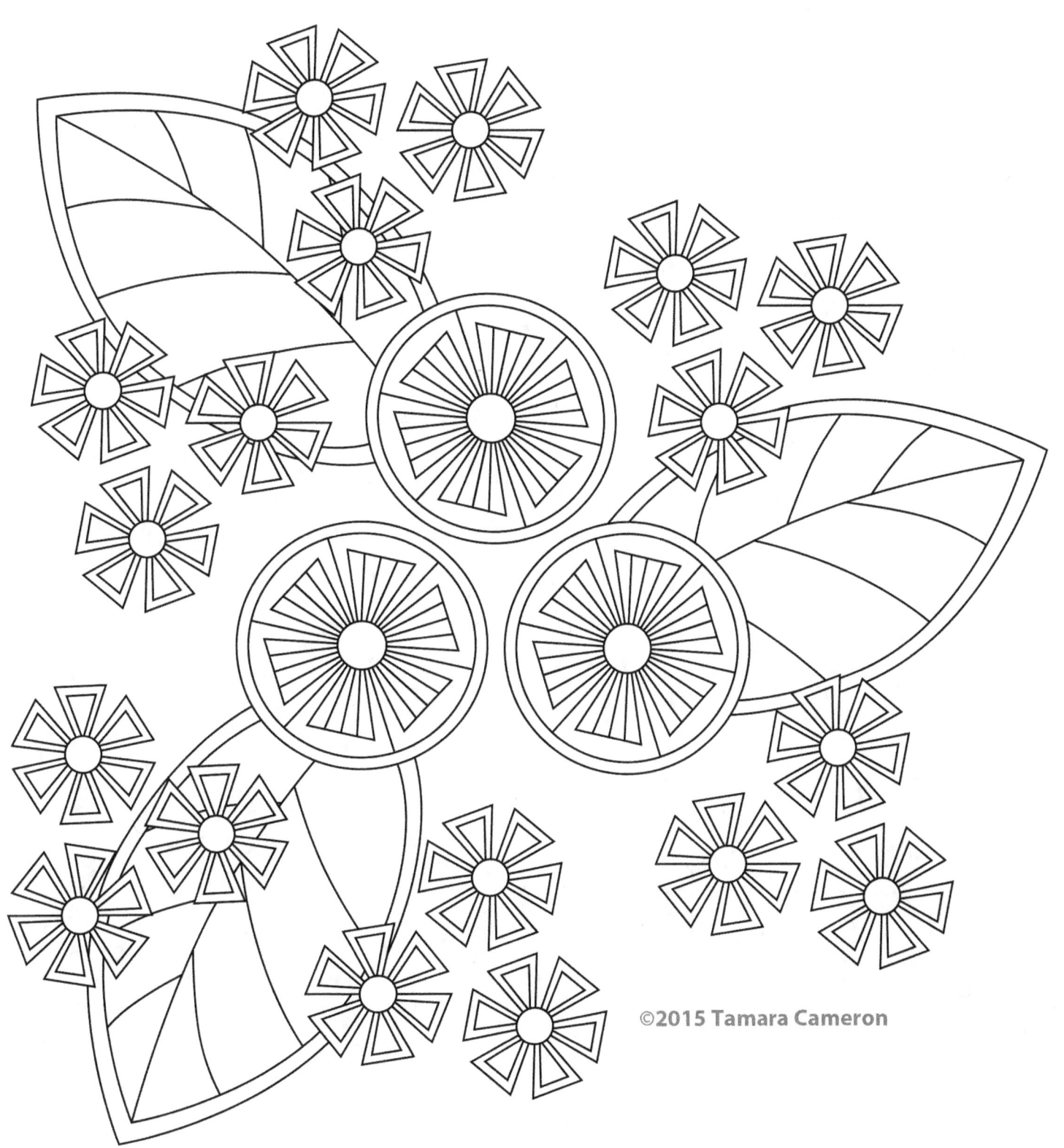
©2015 Tamara Cameron

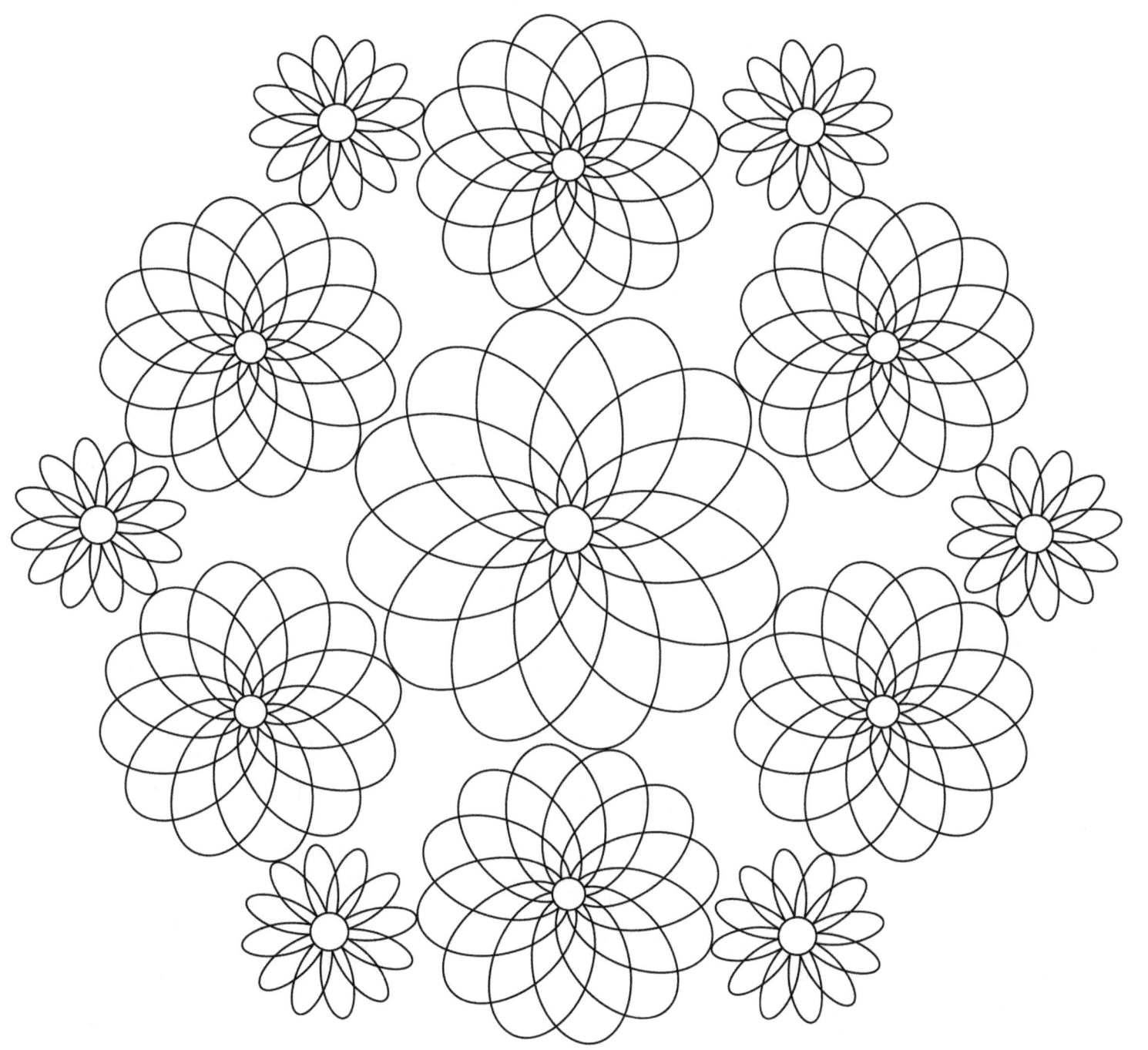

©2015 Tamara Cameron

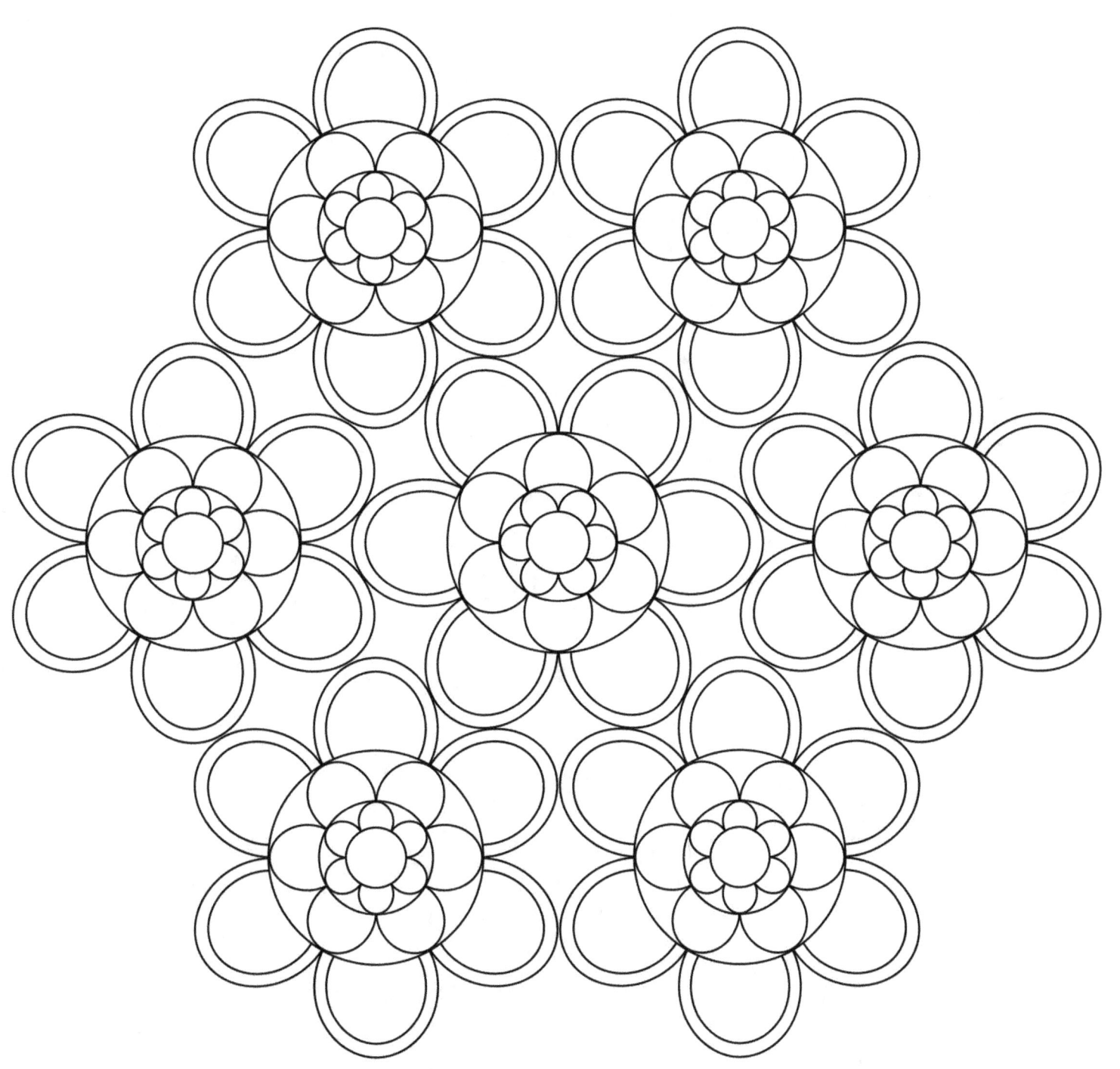
©2015 Tamara Cameron

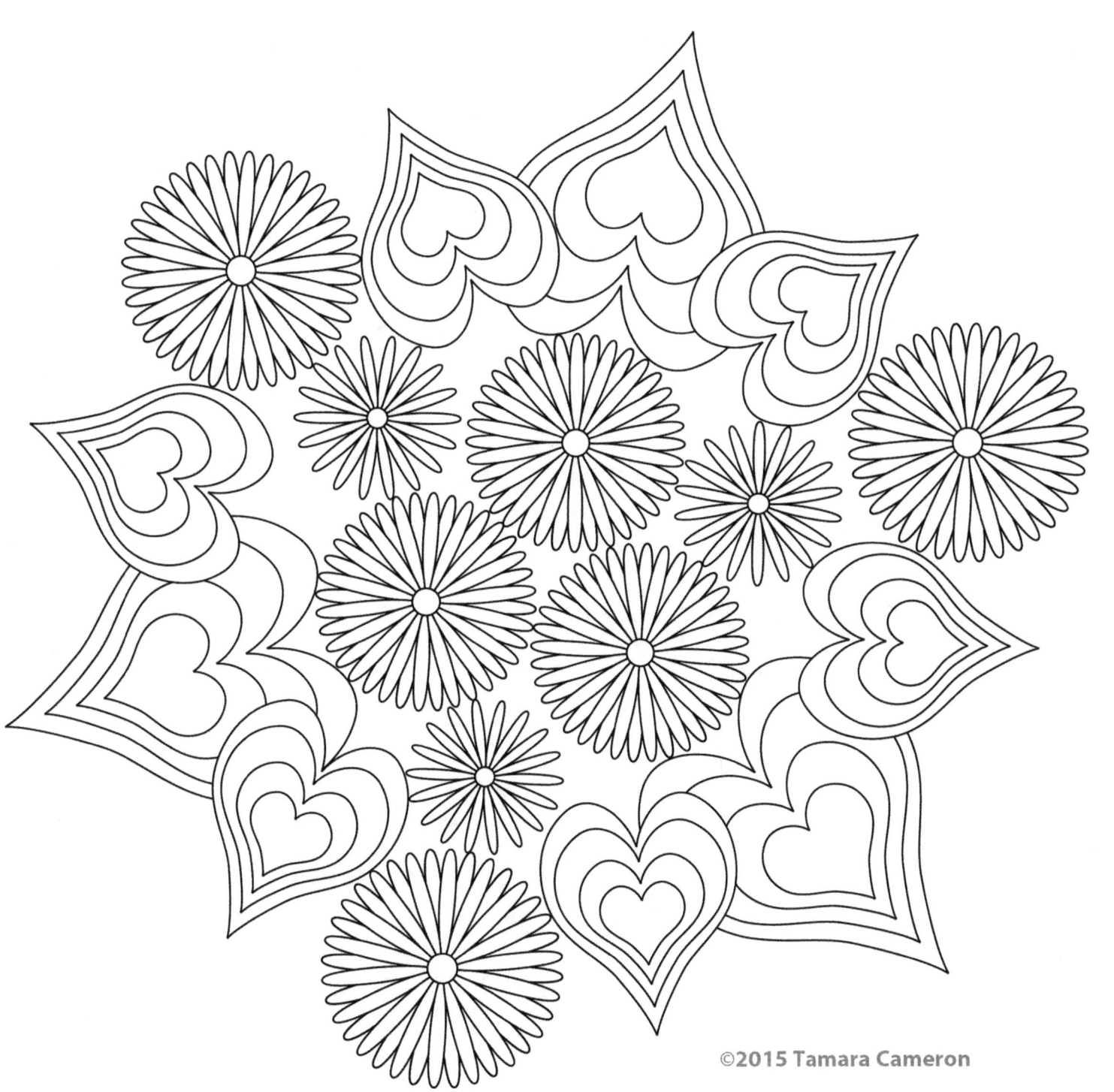

©2015 Tamara Cameron

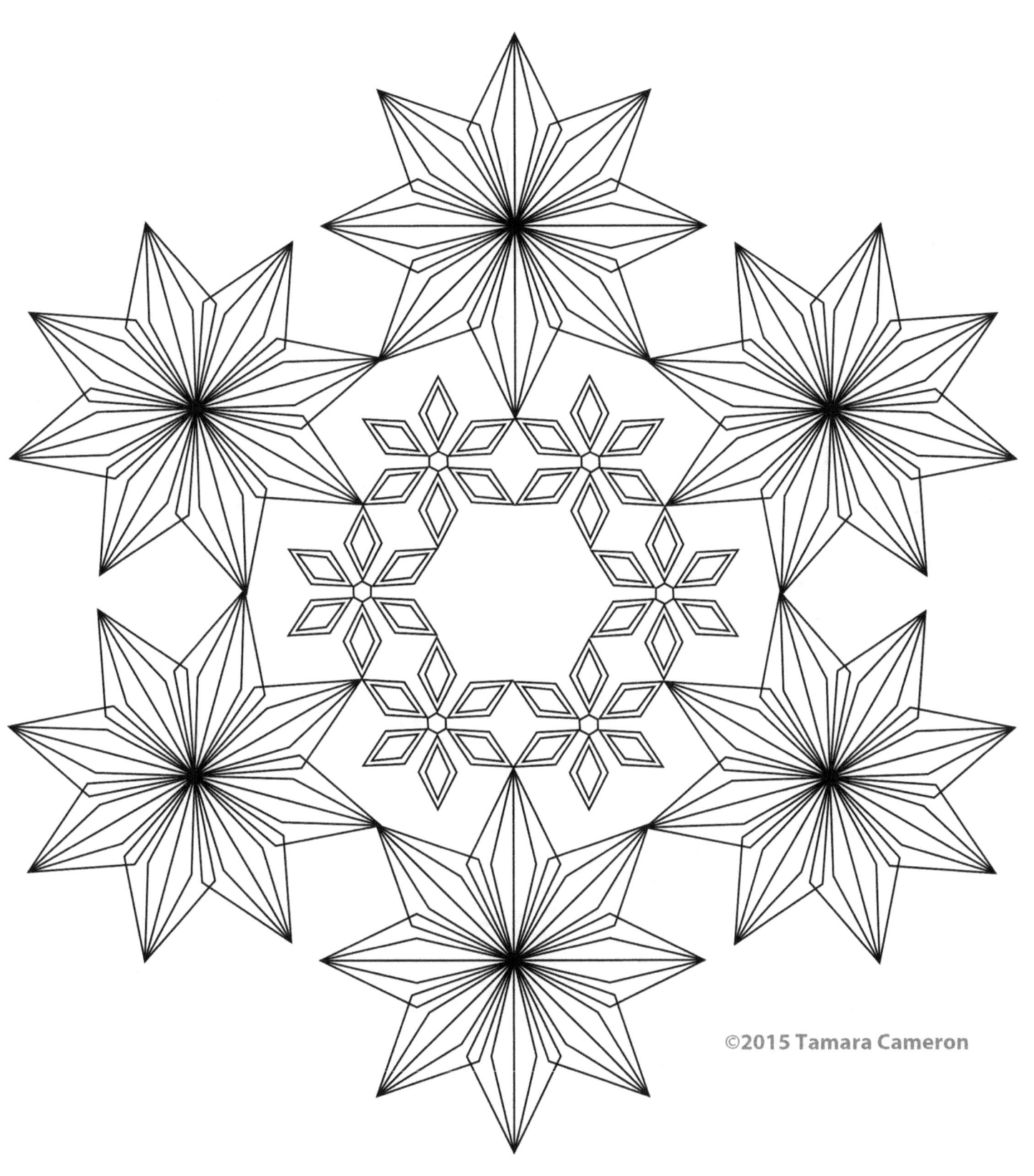

*Contributing Artist*
*Heba Seada*
*Canada*

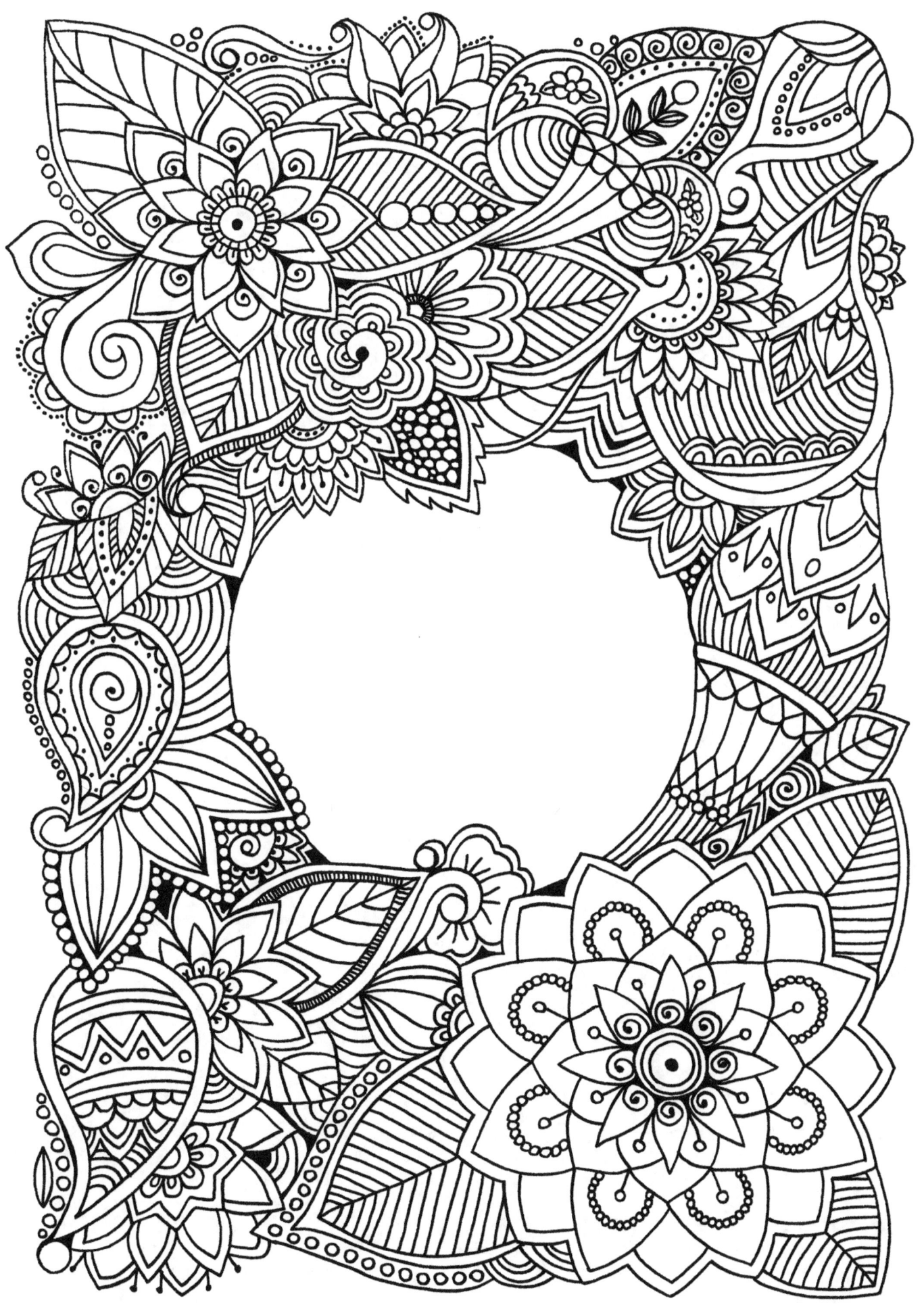

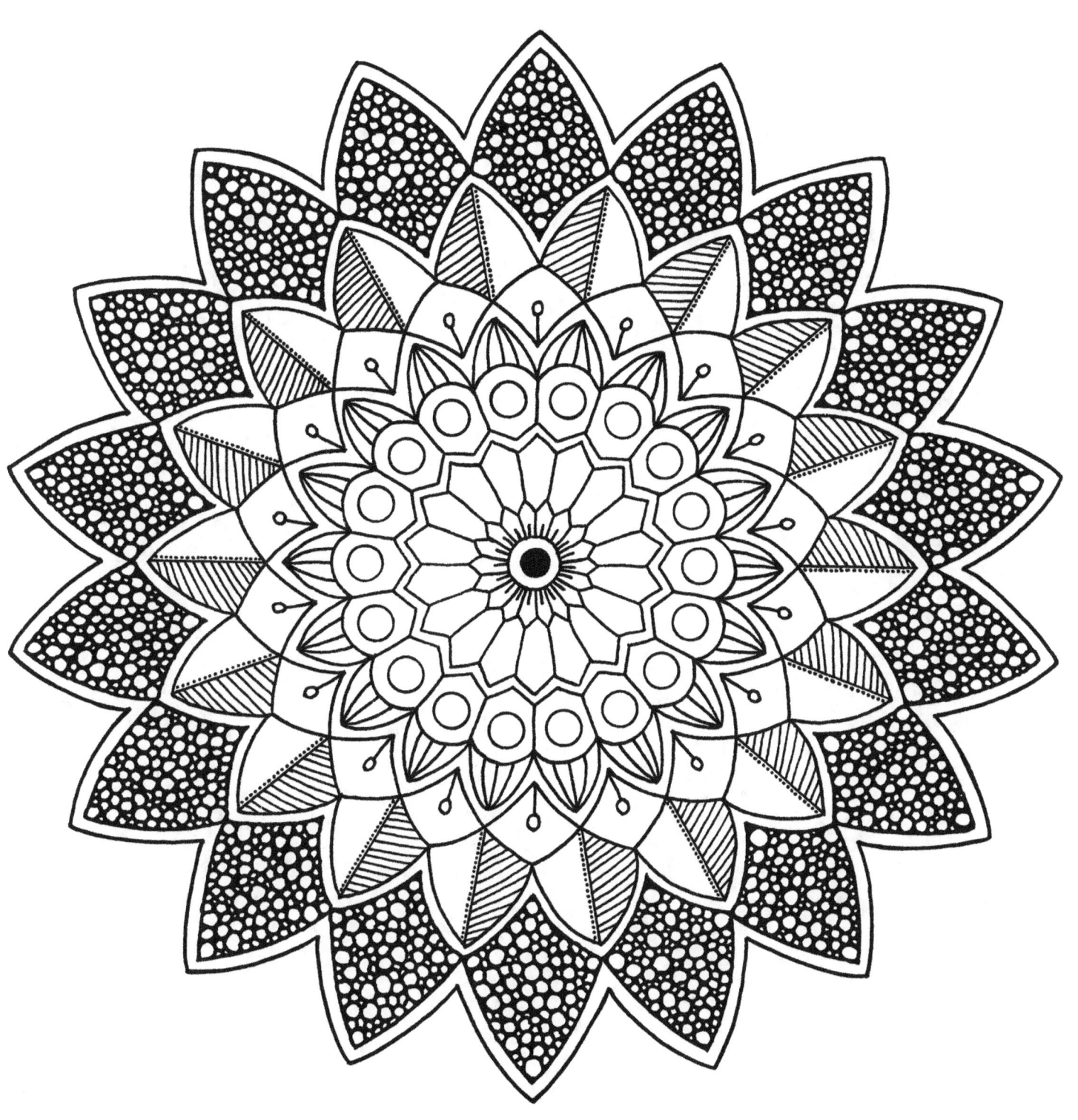

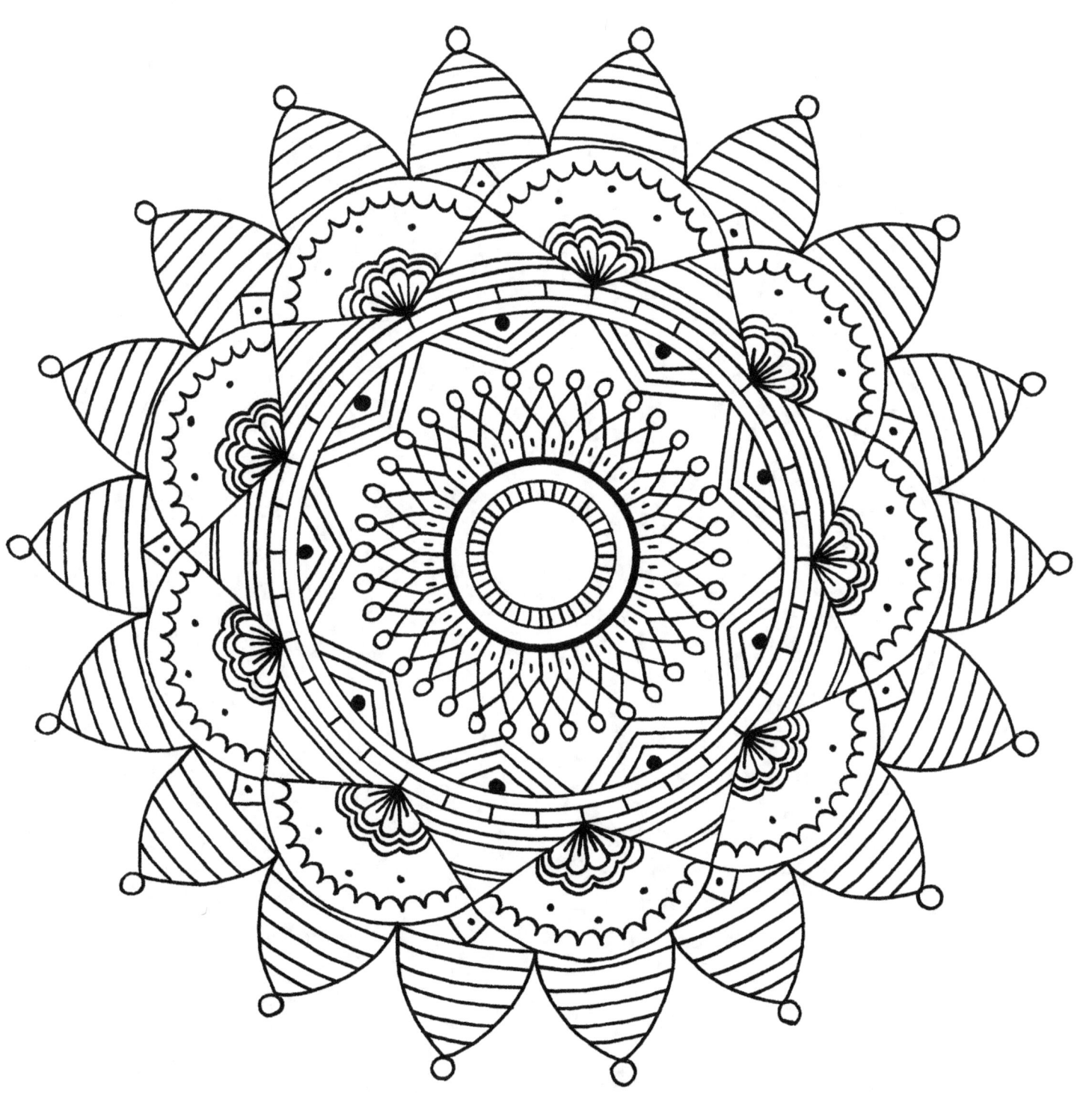

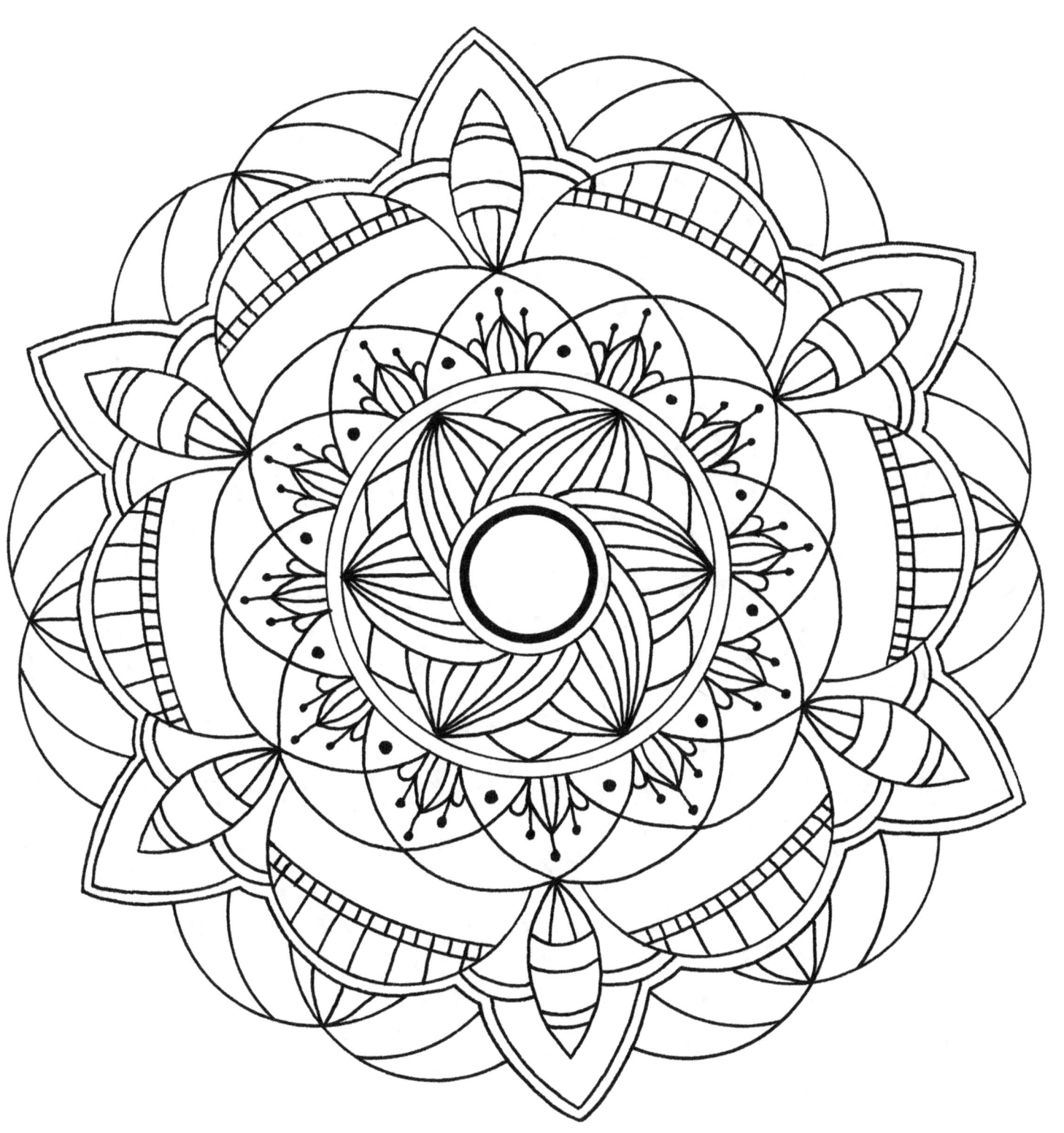

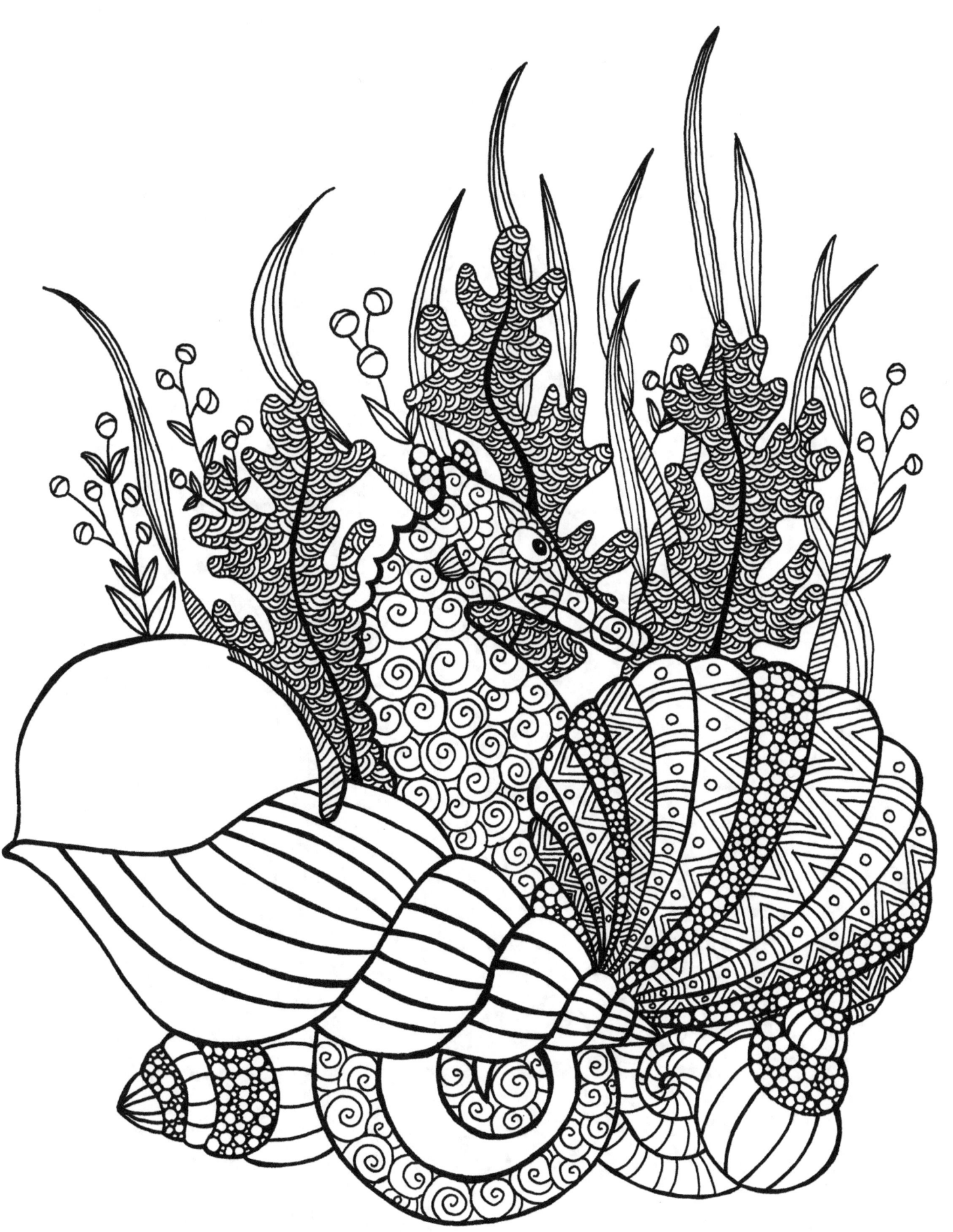

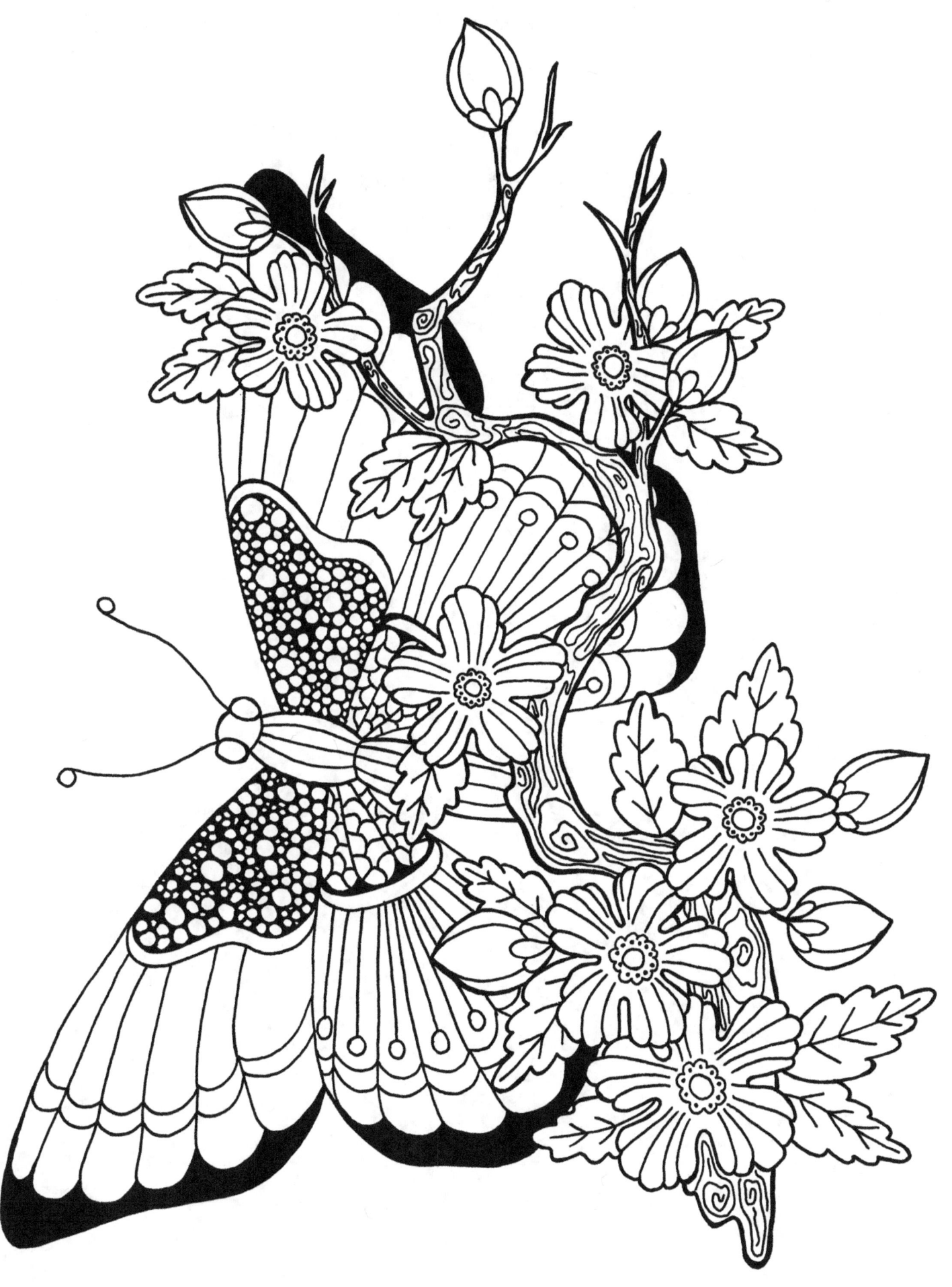

*Contributing Artist*
*Pica Wu*
*Taiwan*

Facebook : Pica's Zentangle Art

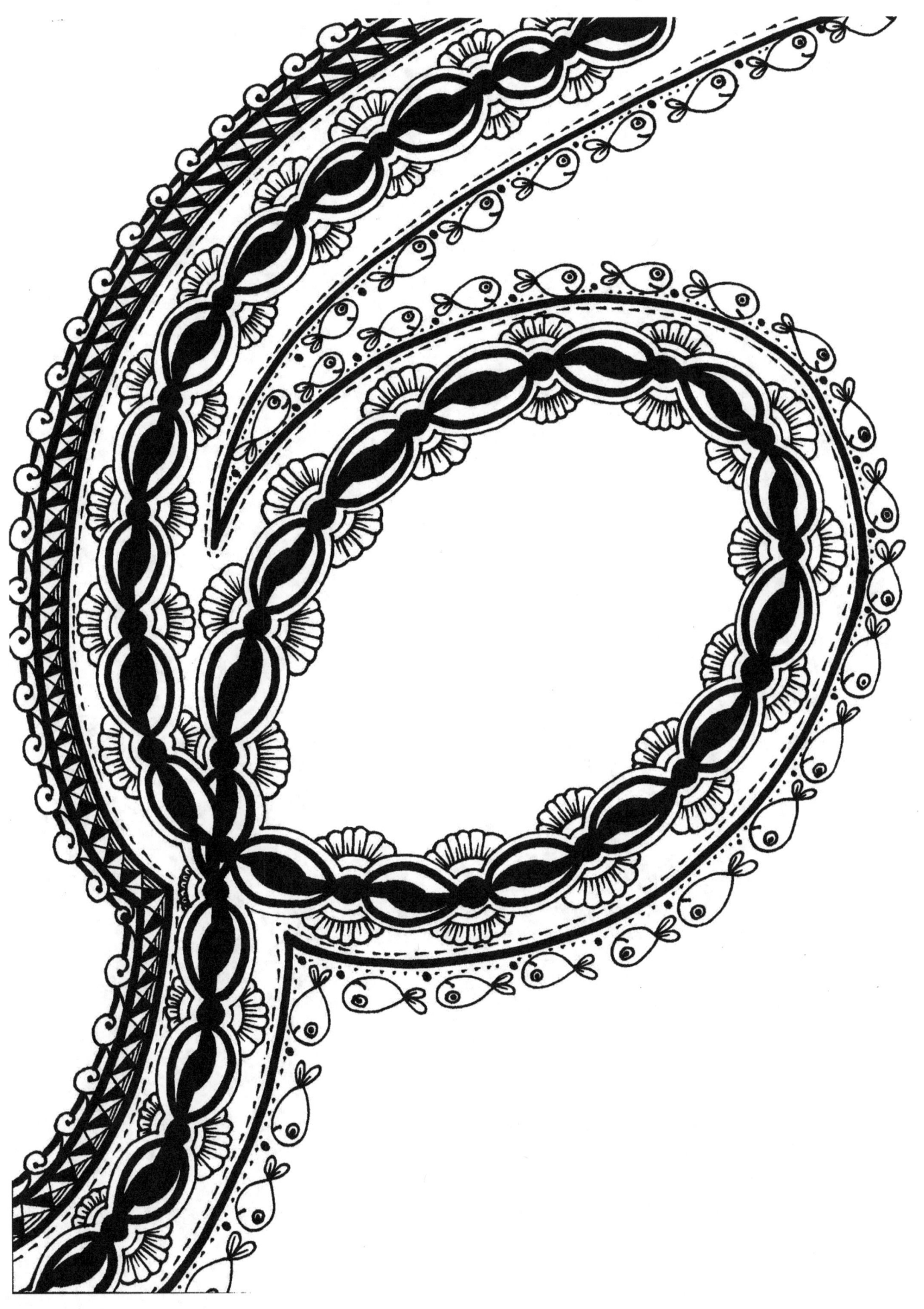

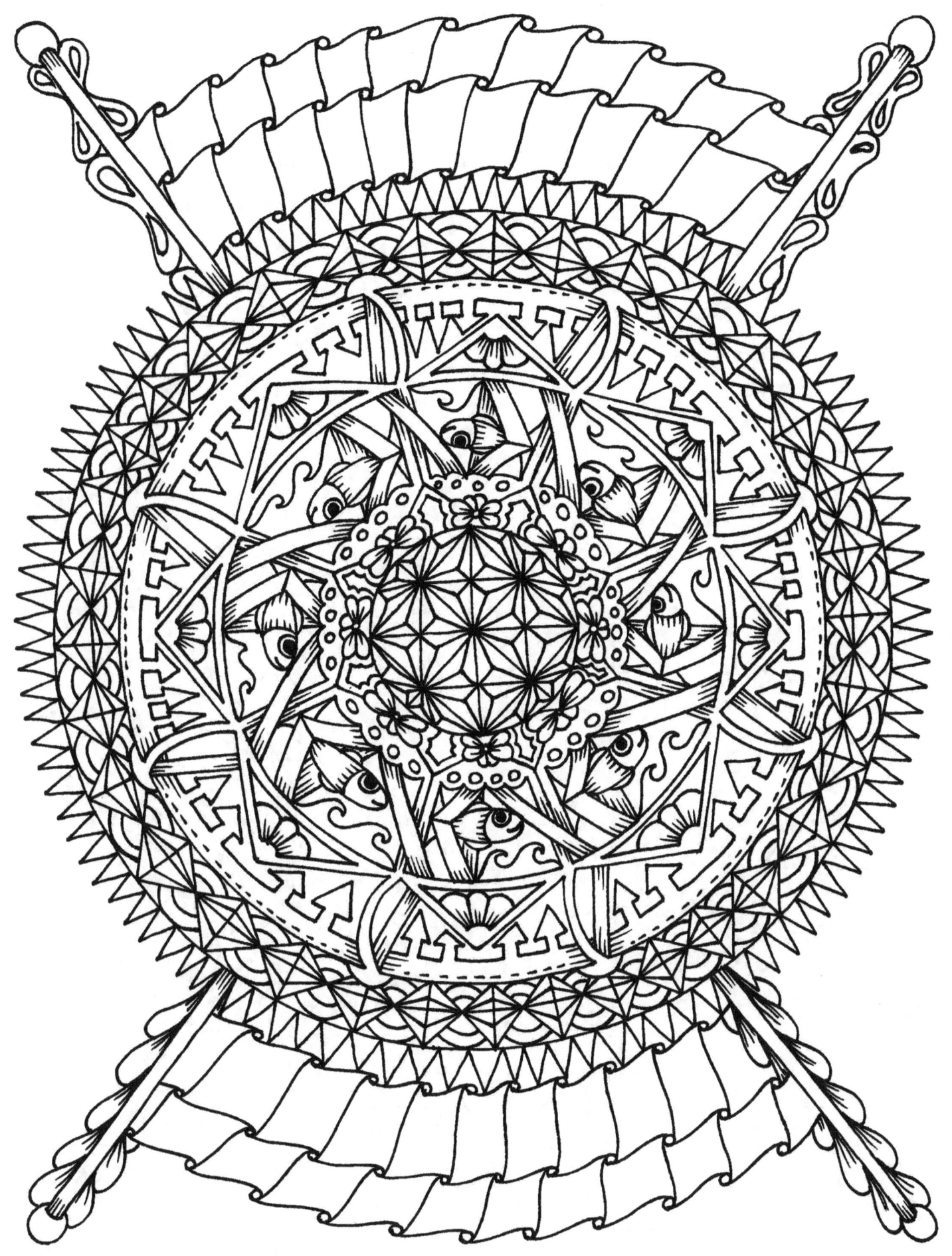

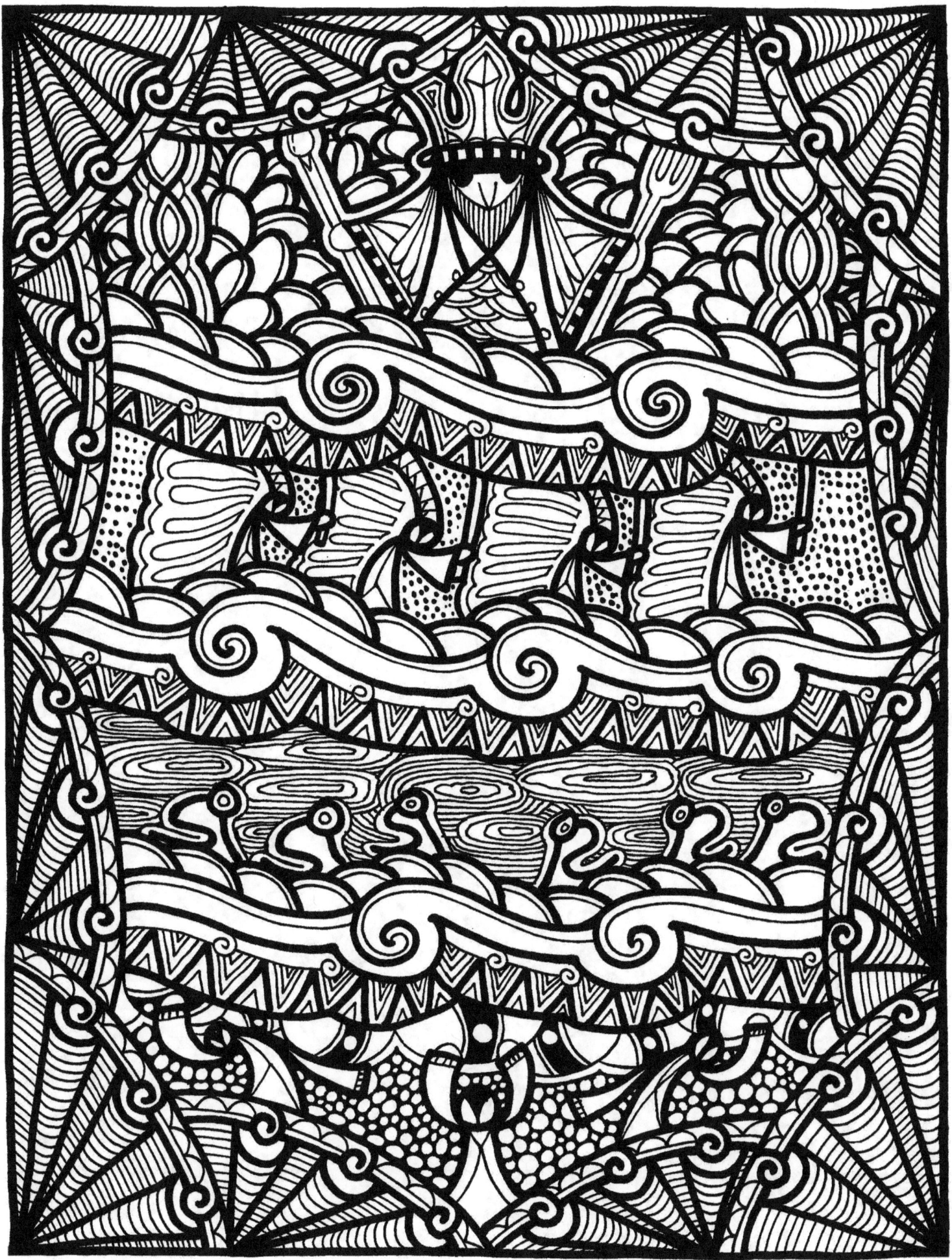

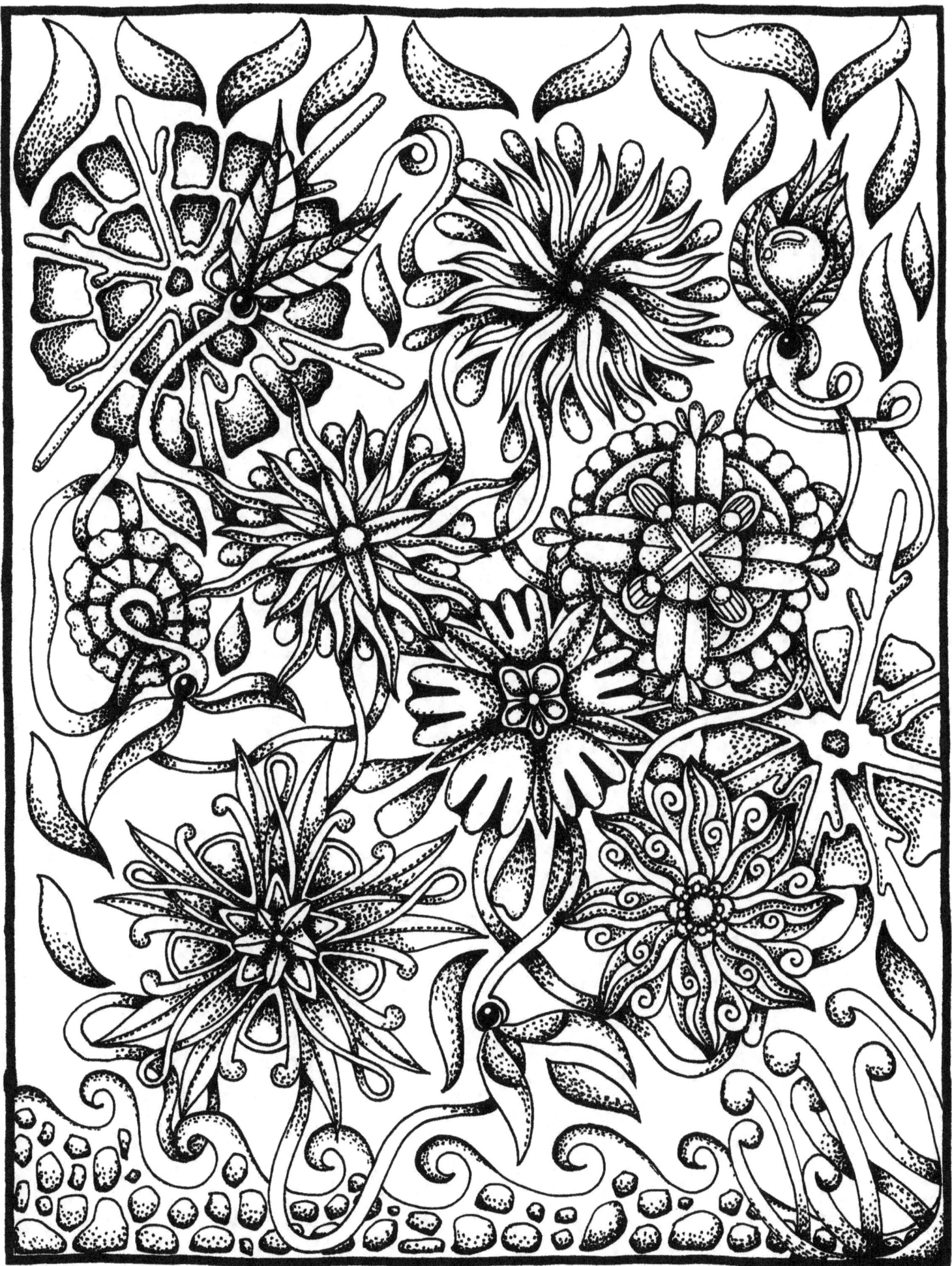

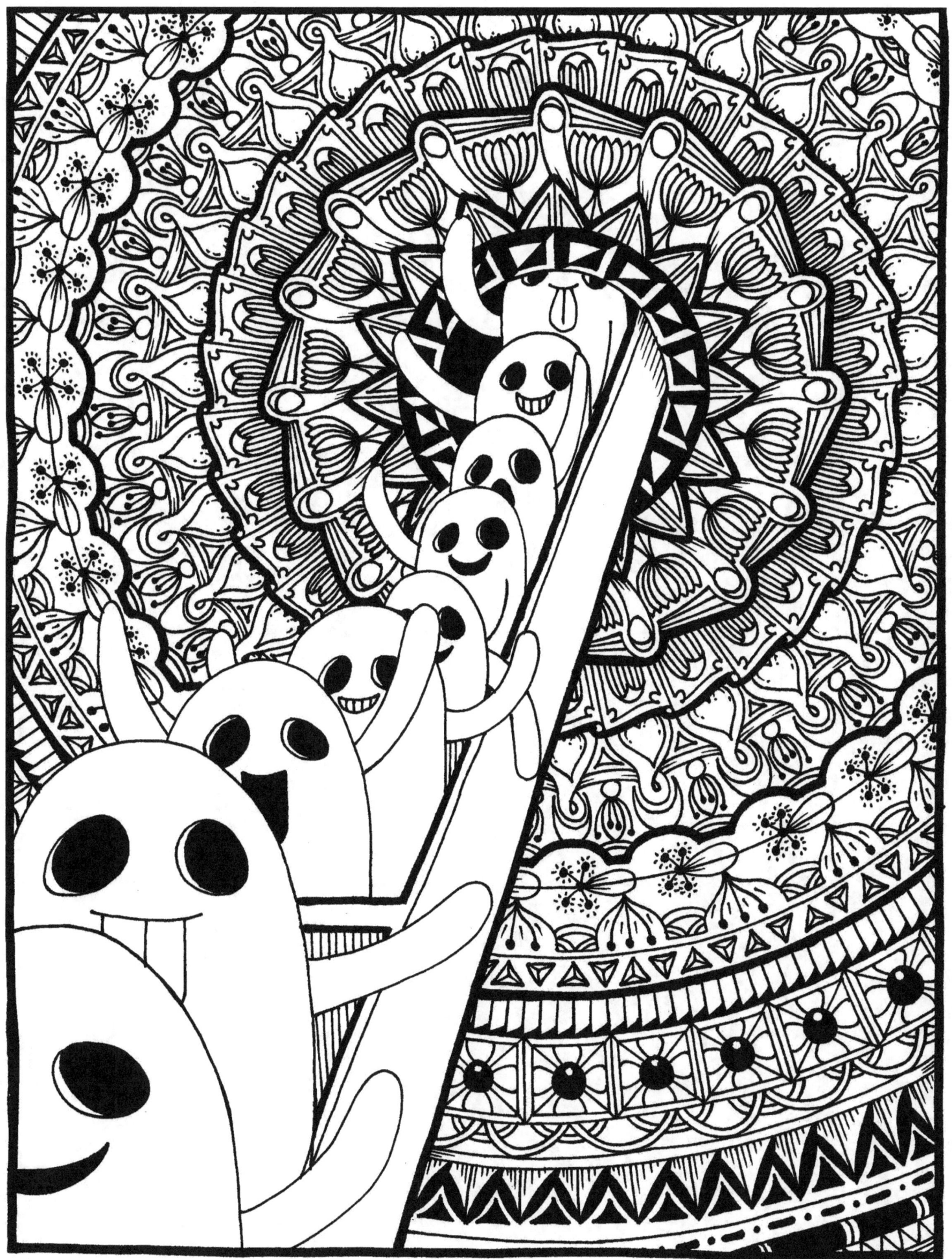

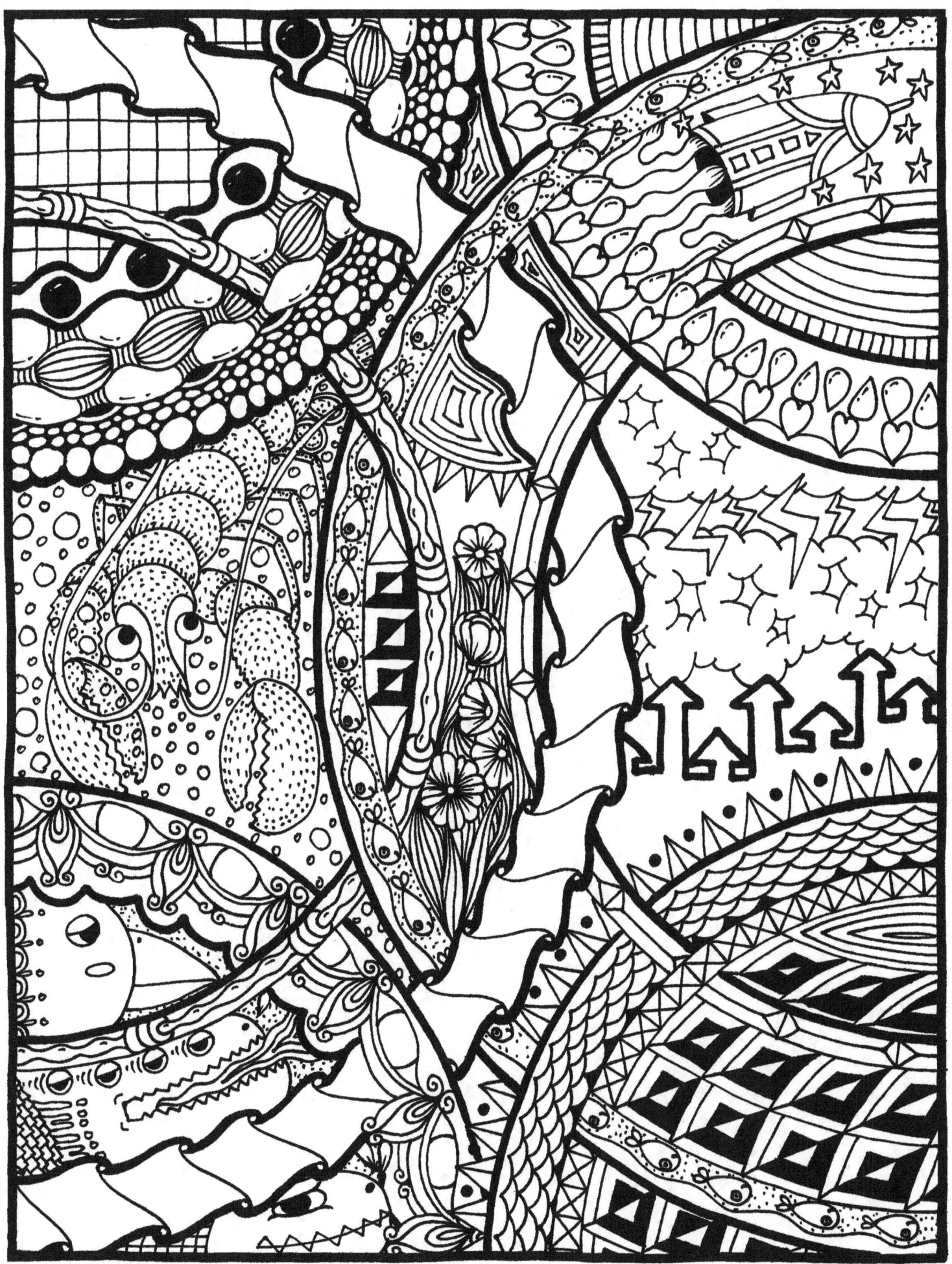

*Contributing Artist*
*Gemeta Ling*
*Germany*

Facebook : Gemeta Ling

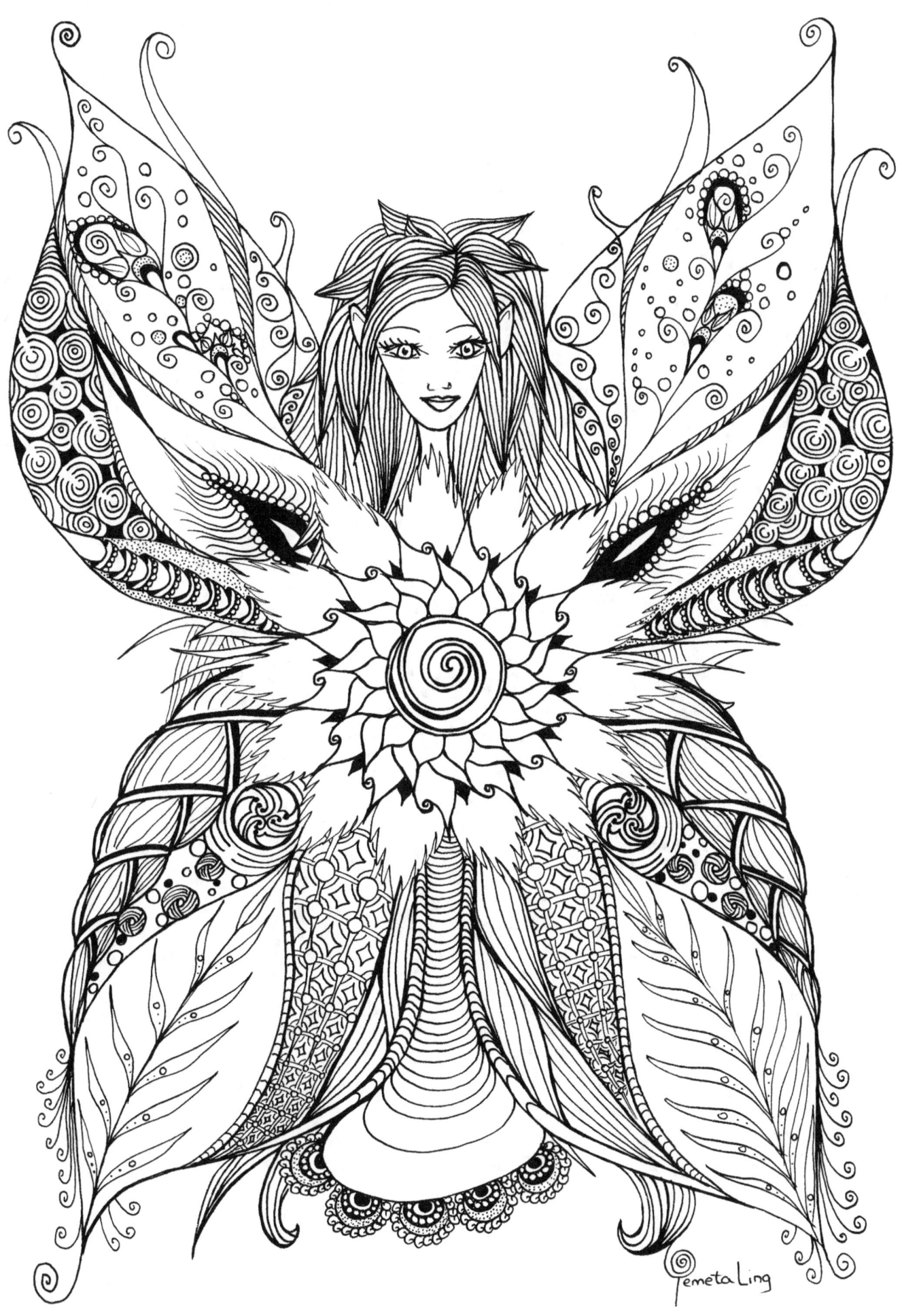

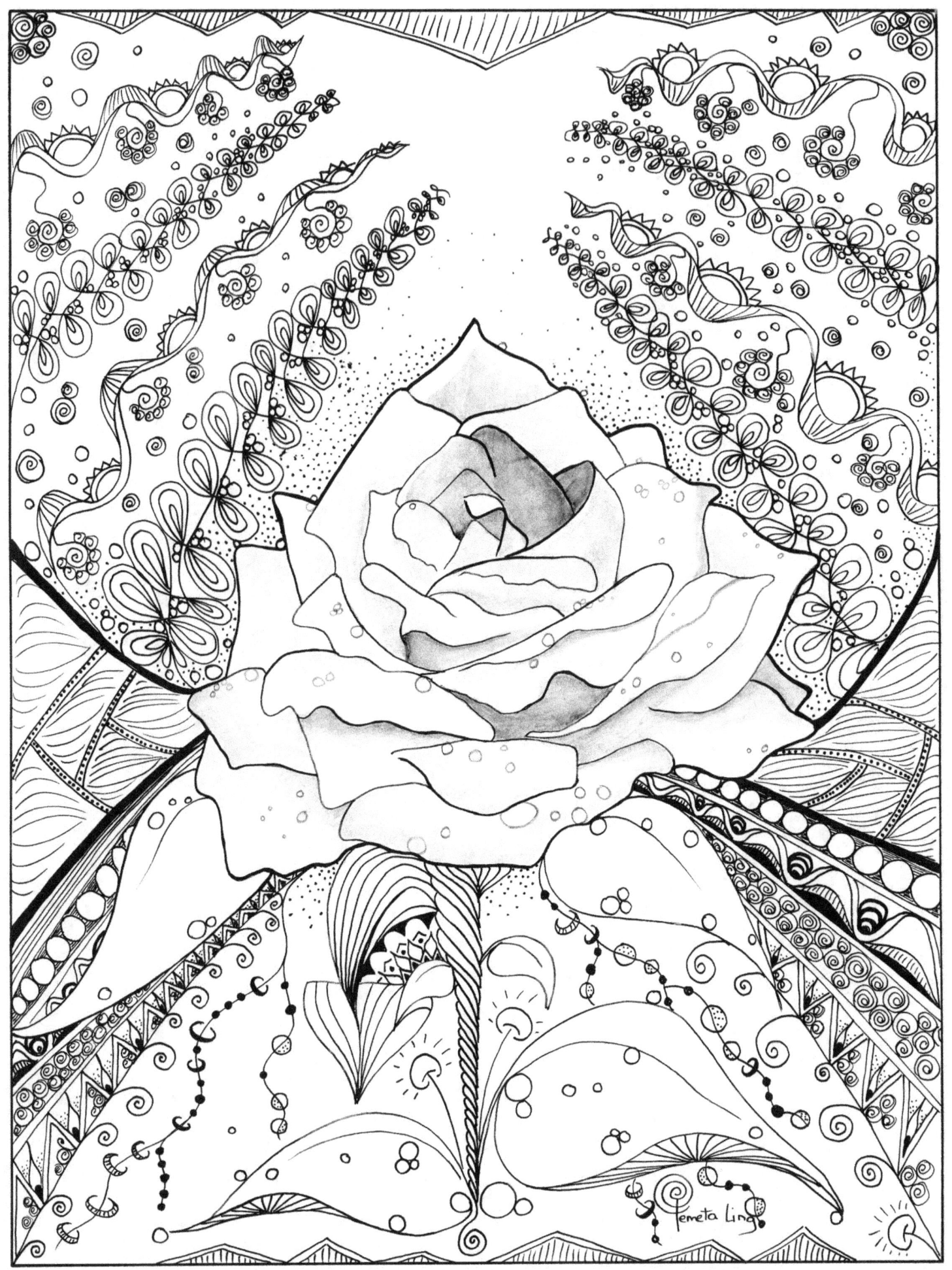

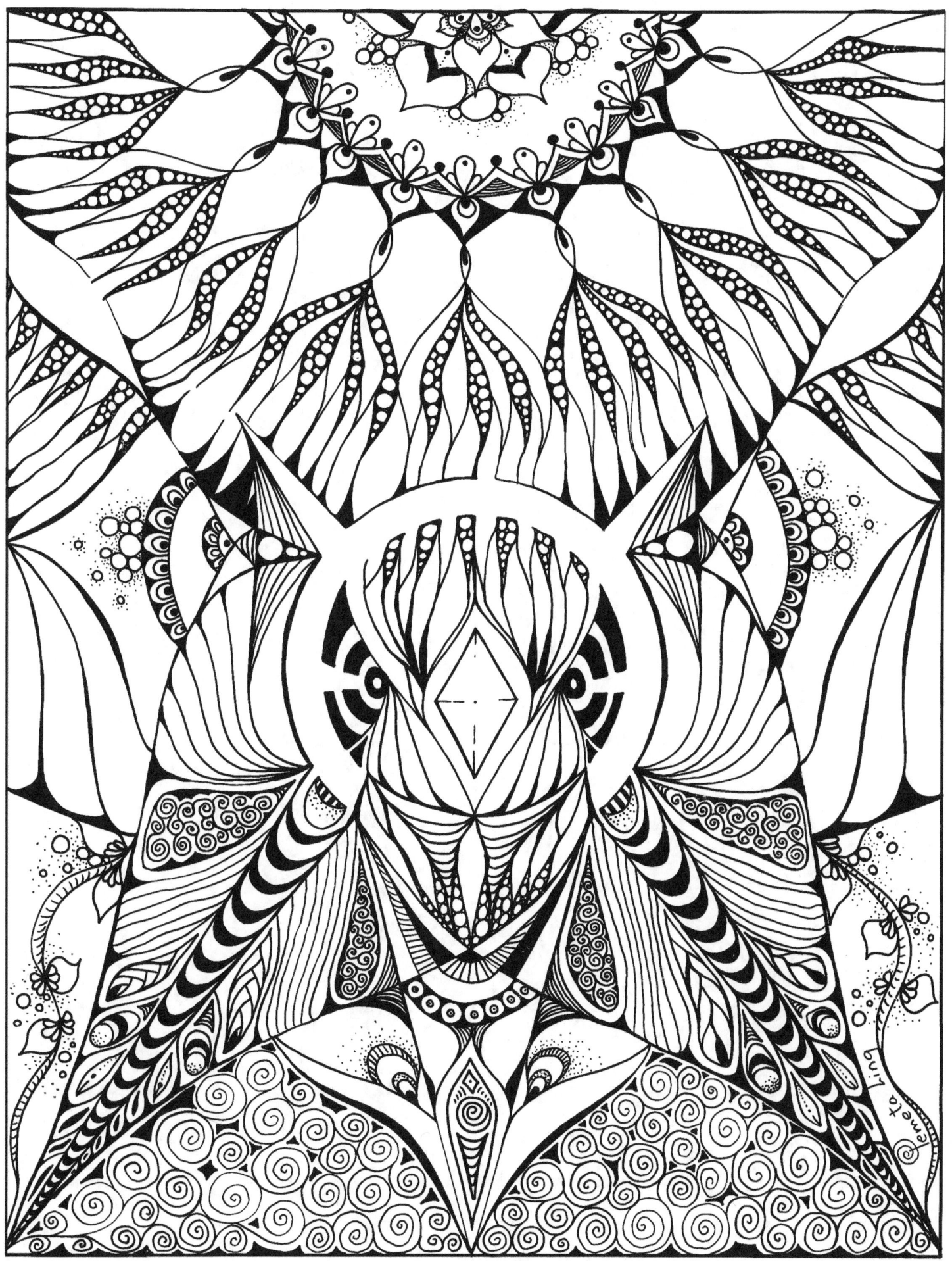

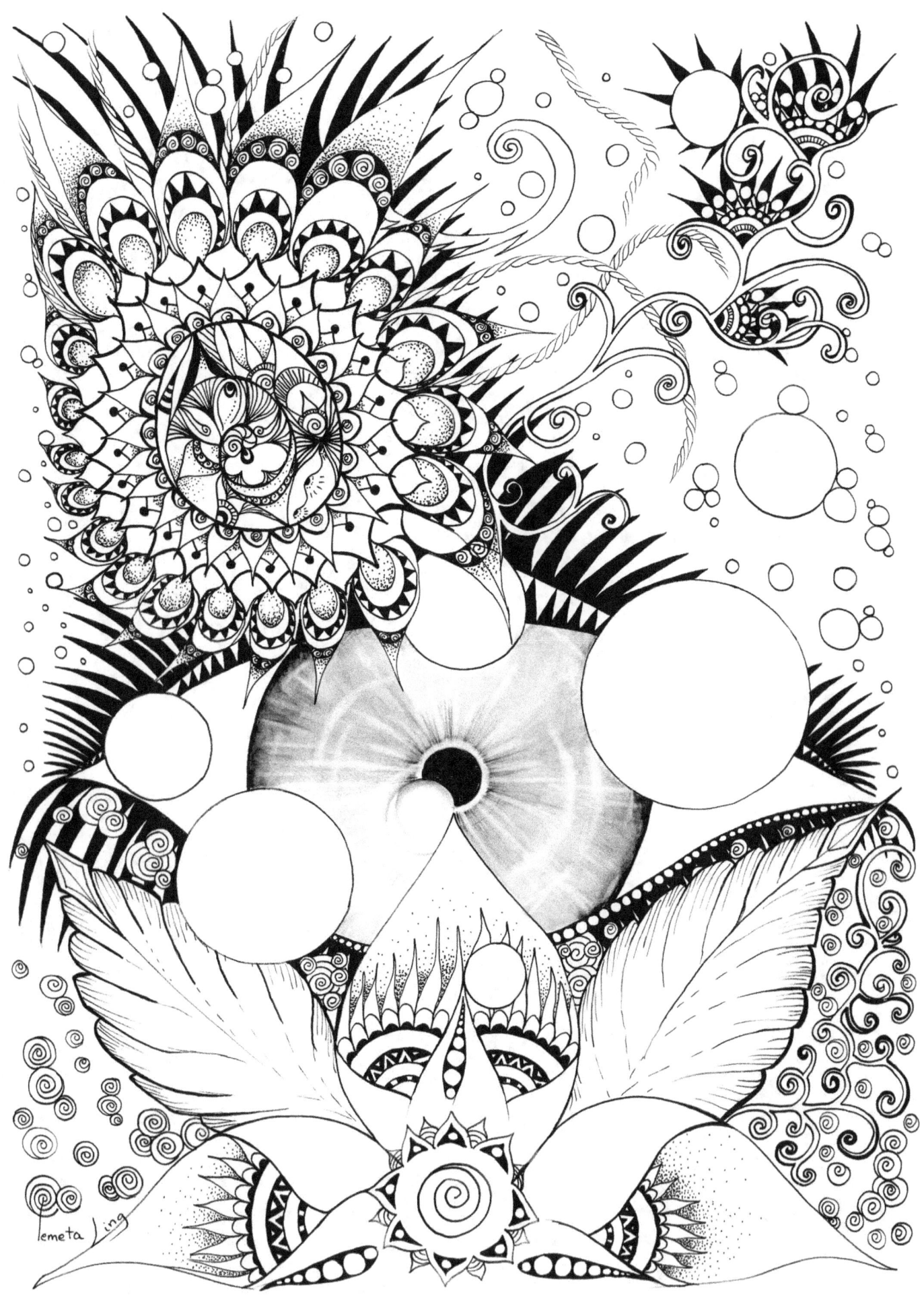

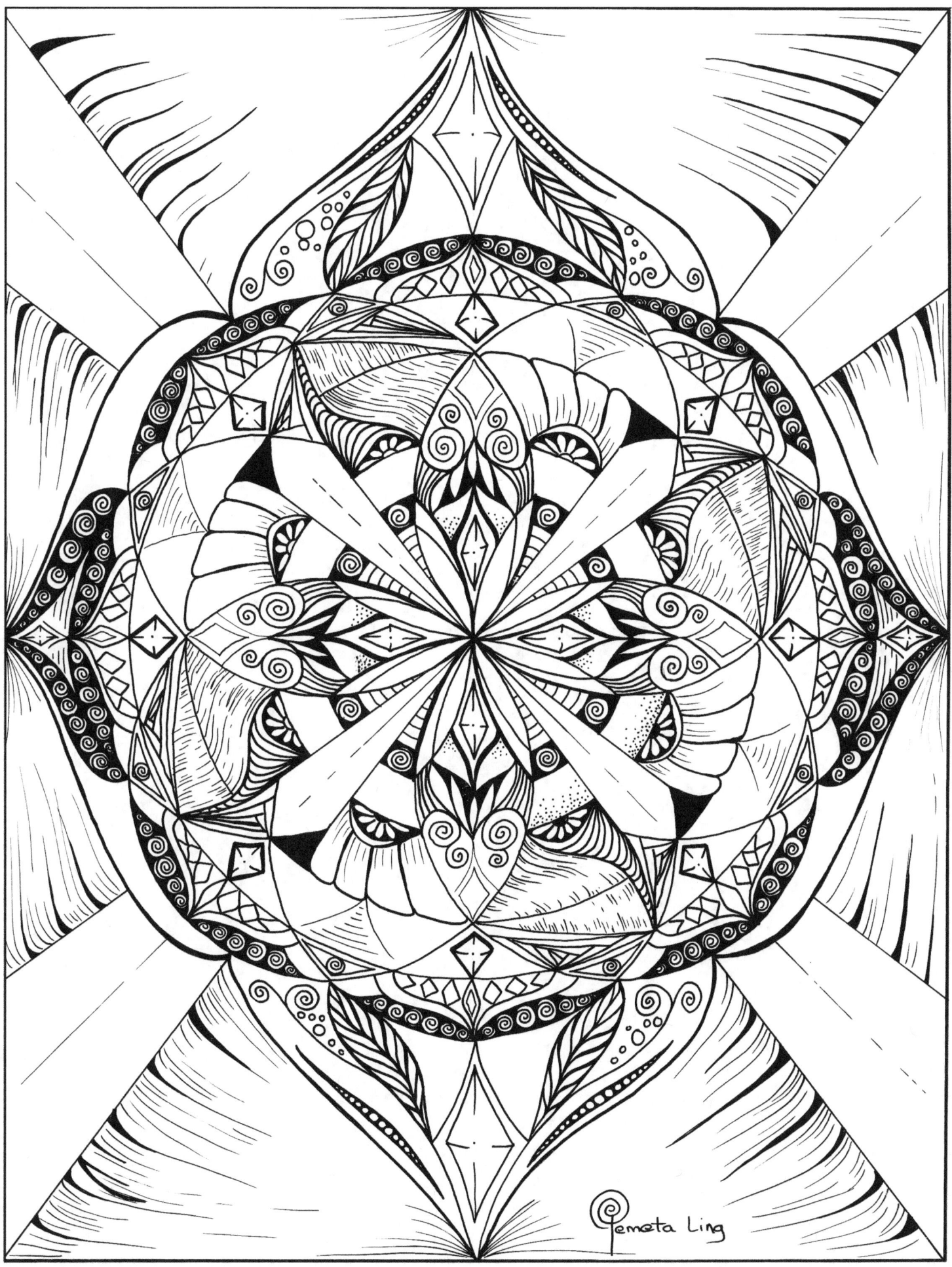

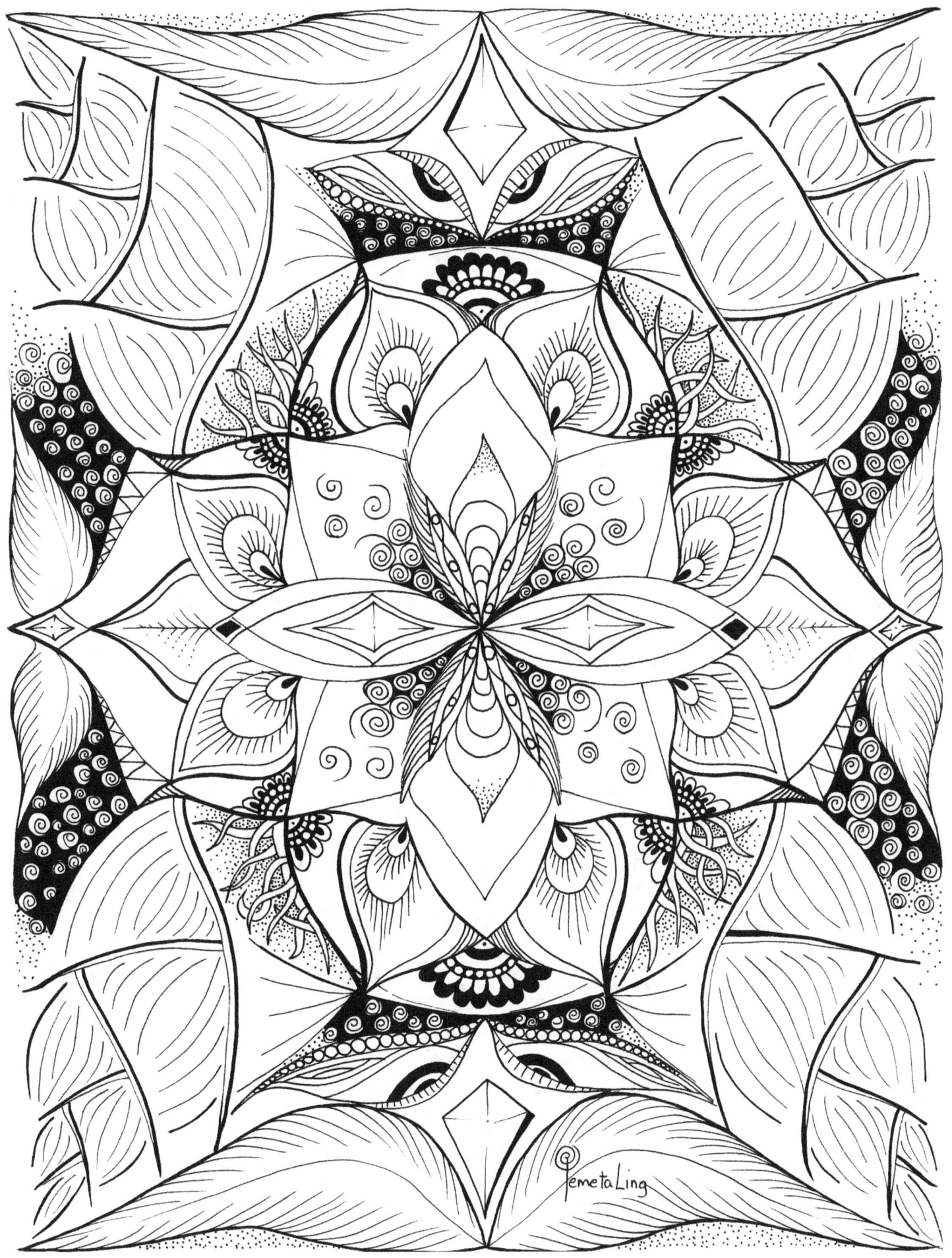

*Contributing Artist*
*KaLoo Design*
*France*

Facebook : KaLoo Design Art

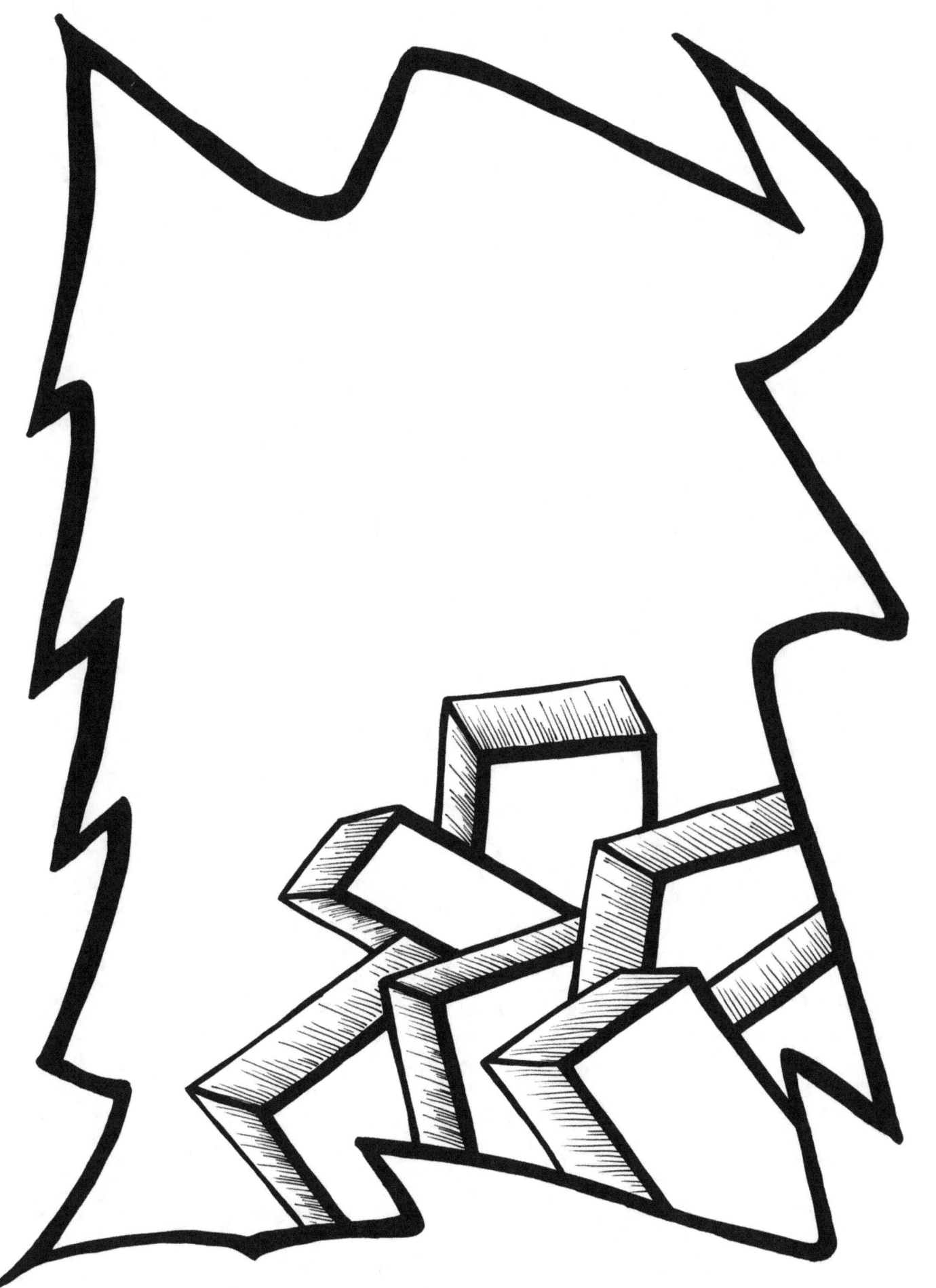

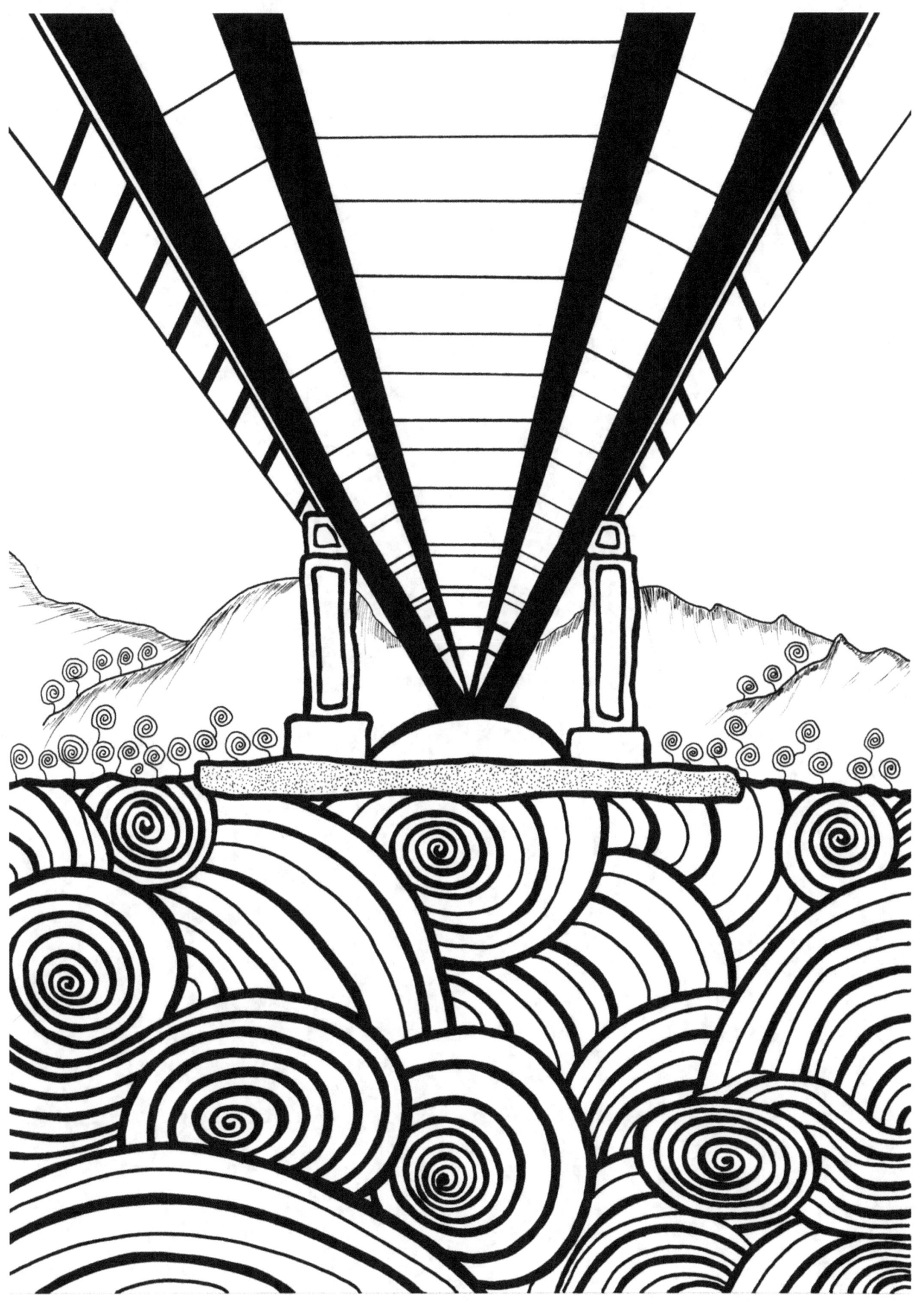

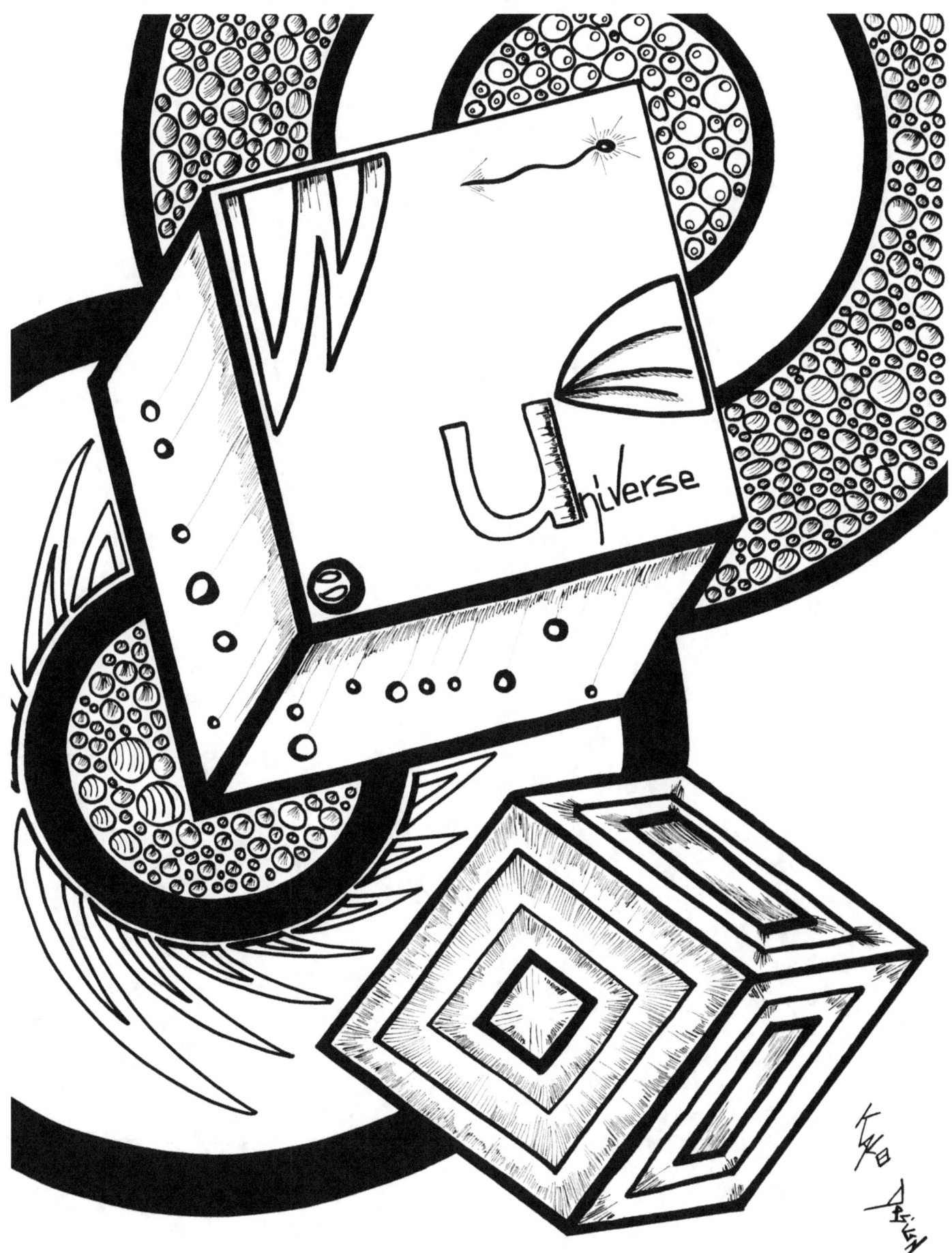

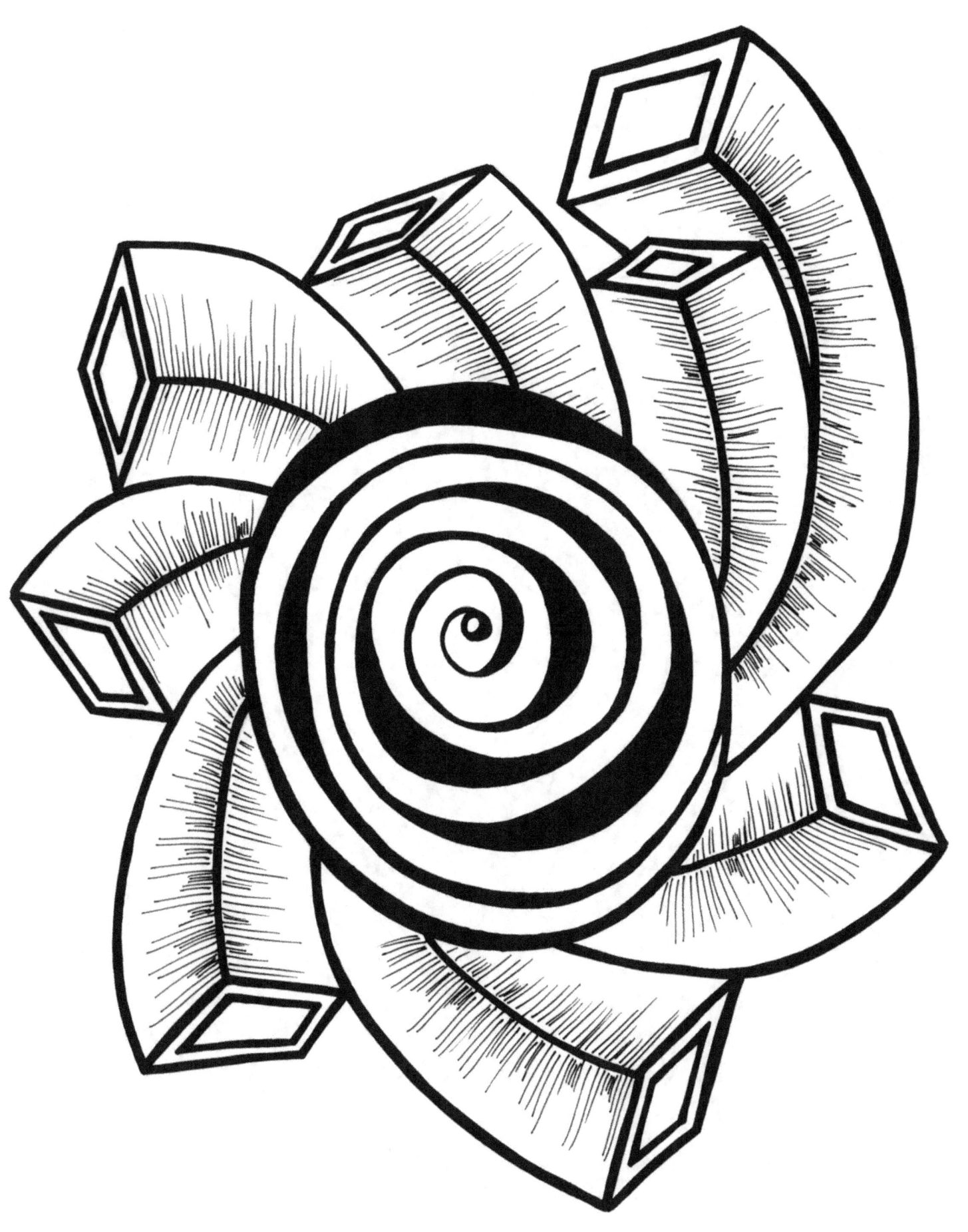

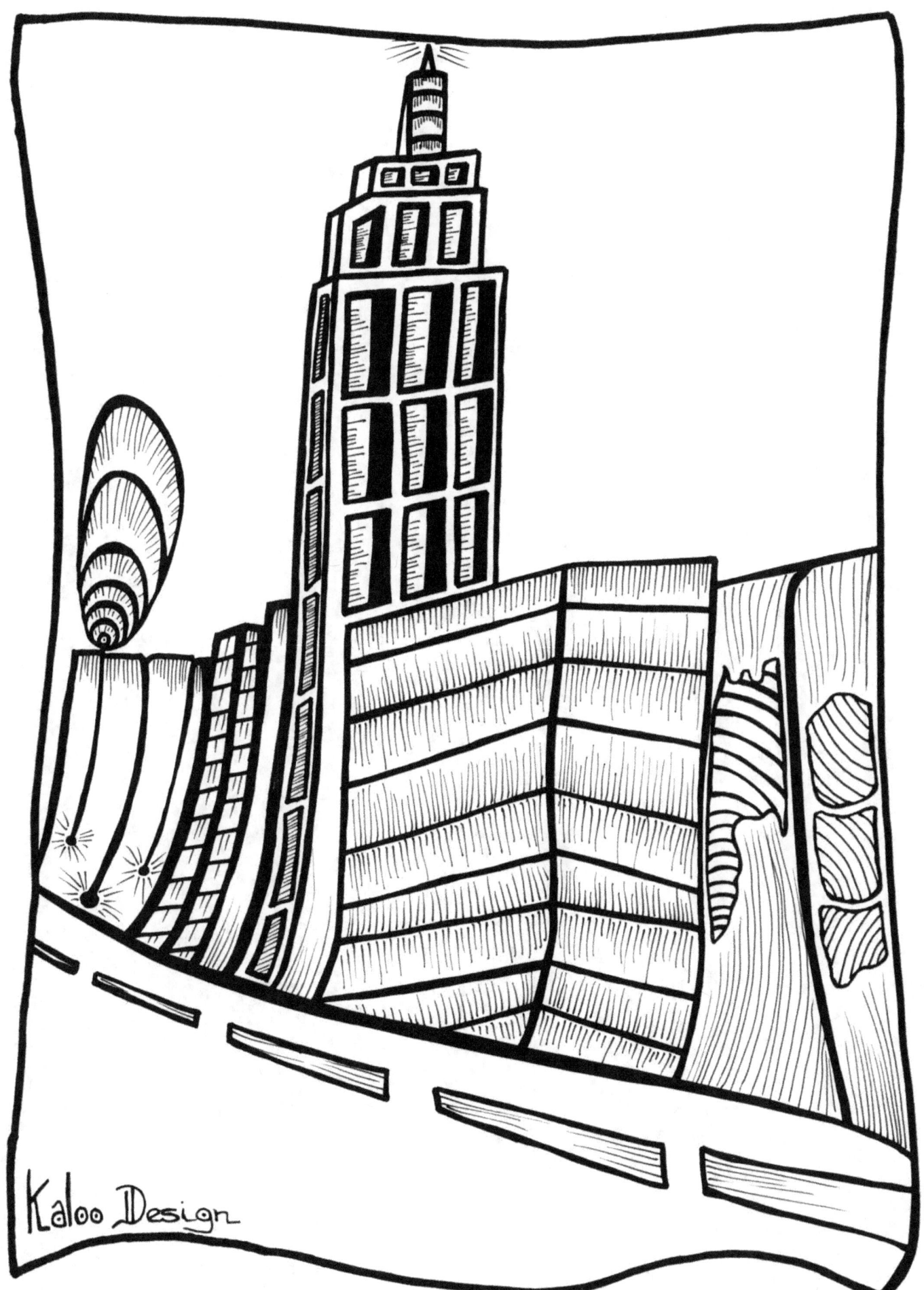

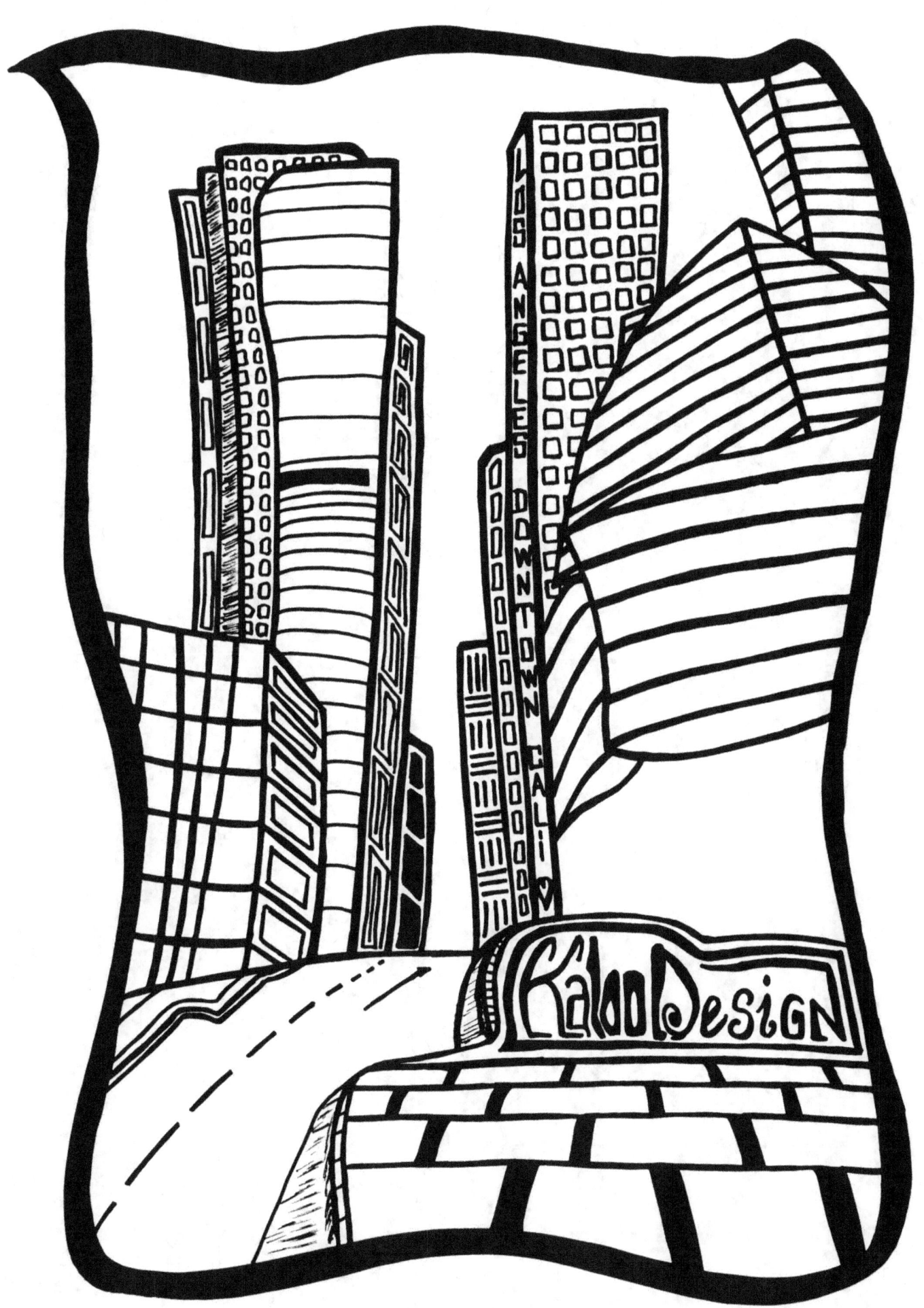

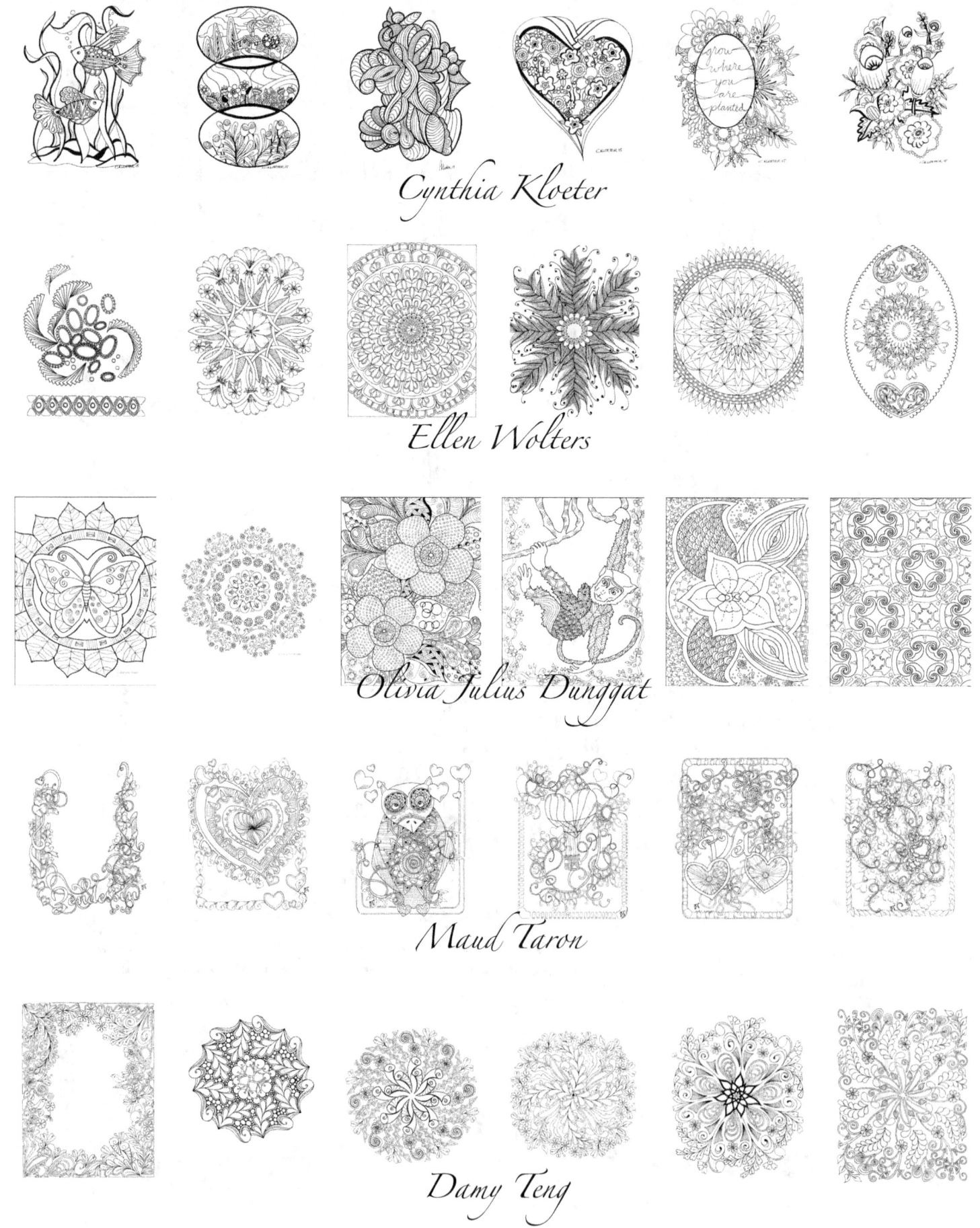

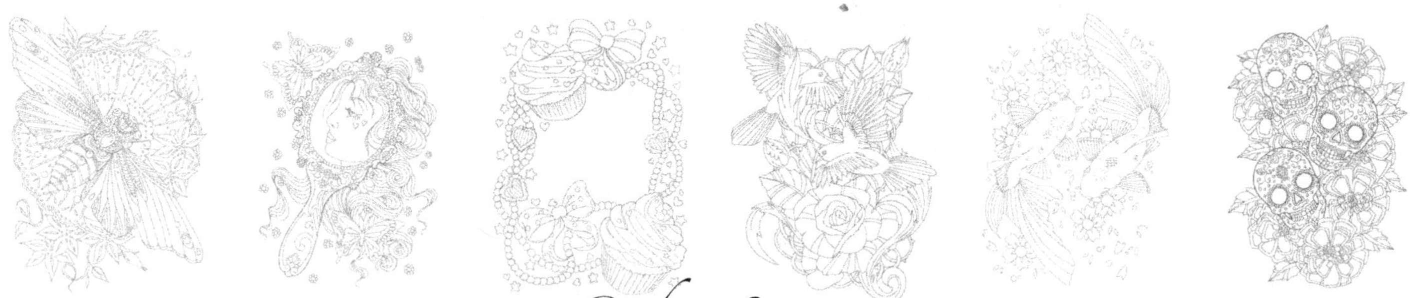

Ondine Summers

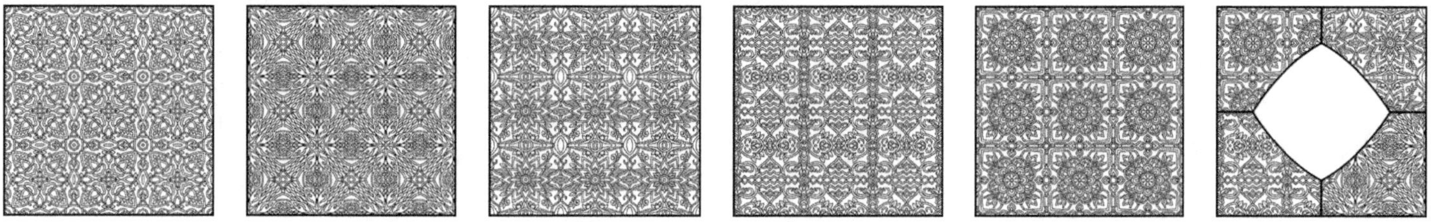

Karim Benyagoub

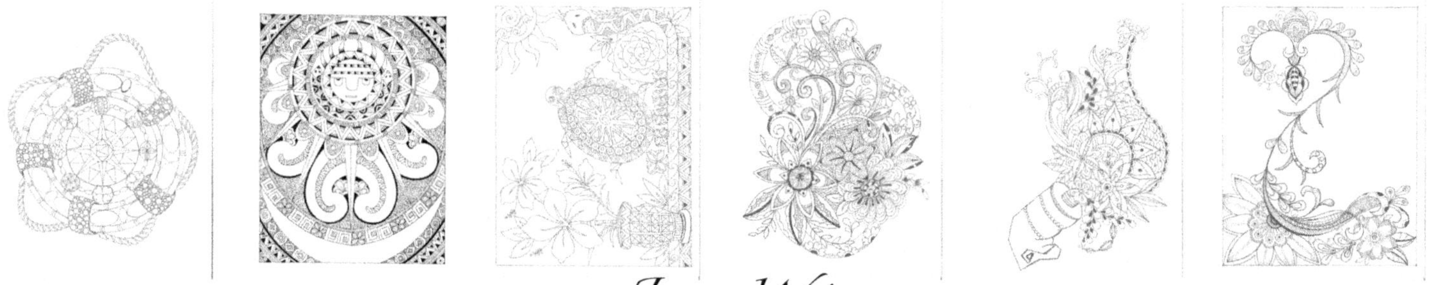

Jenny Wei

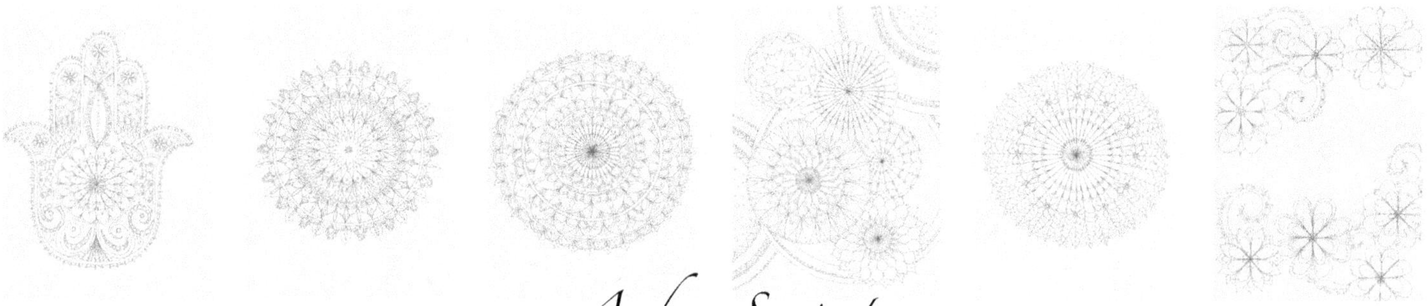

Andrea Sargent

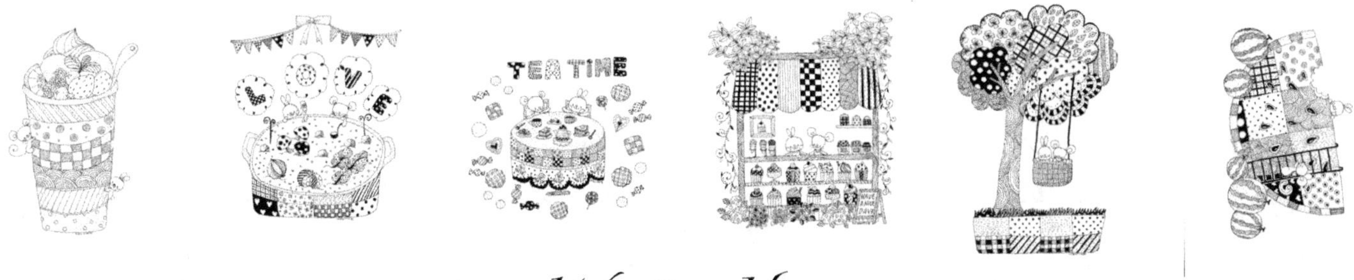

Wanting Huang

*Test your colors here on the samples from*
*"My Pocket Coloring Companion"*
*&*
*"My Coloring Companion"*

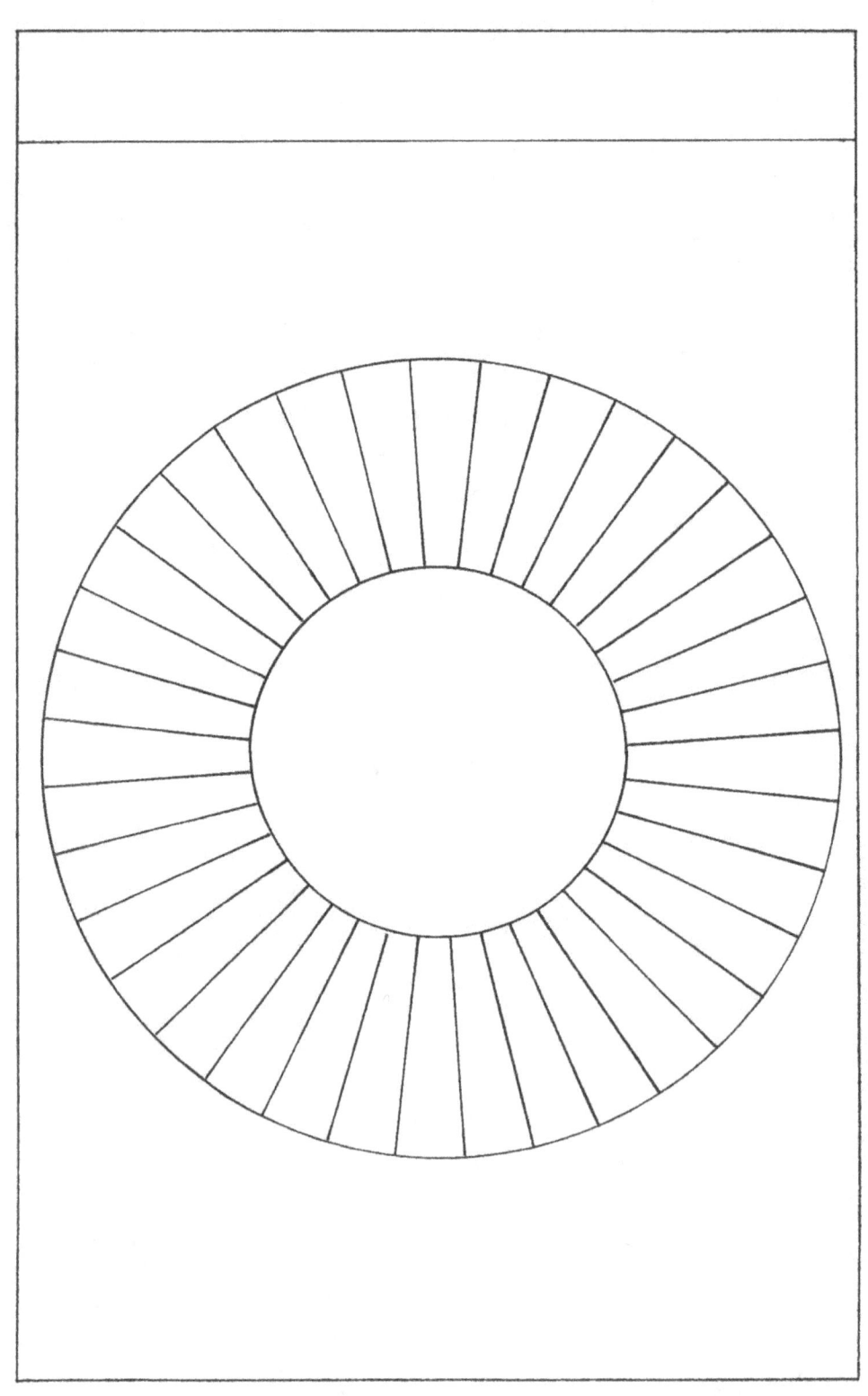

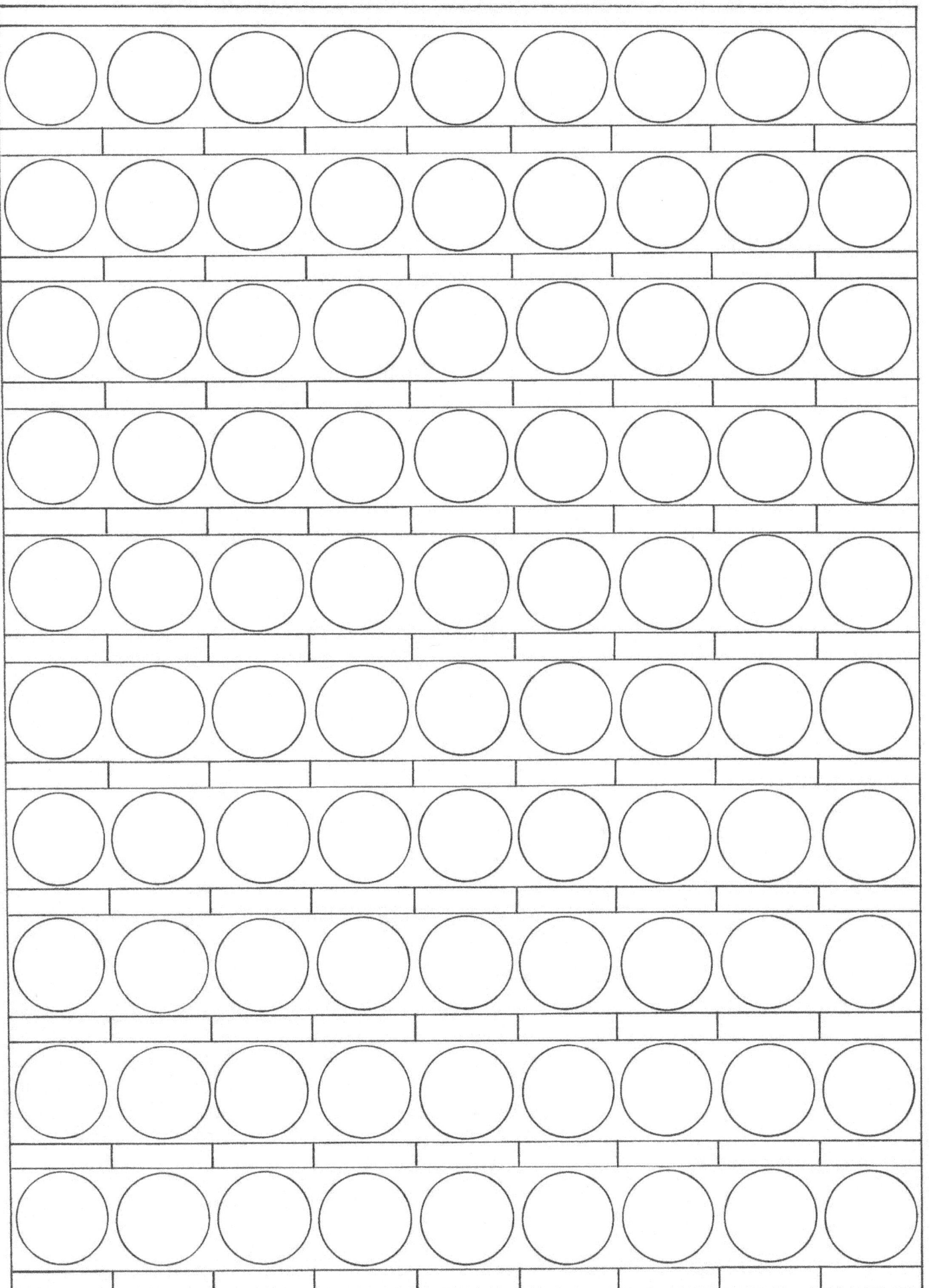

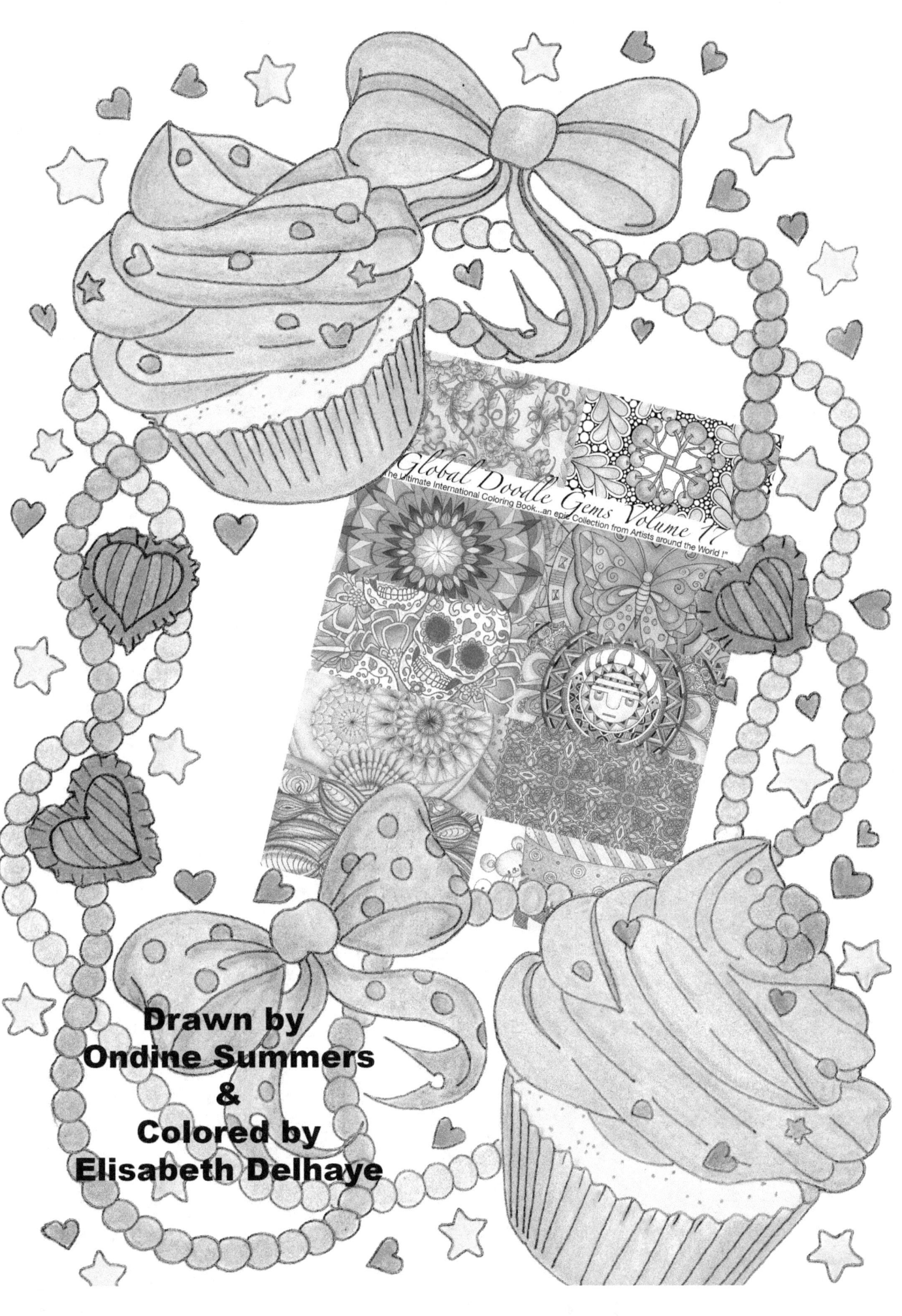

www.ingramcontent.com/pod-product-compliance
Lightning Source LLC
Chambersburg PA
CBHW082208220526
45470CB00010B/3081